At the age of six years.

"How delightful it will be to go up to that Heaven and see God who never dies."

THE

PERSIAN FLOWER:

A

MEMOIR

OF

JUDITH GRANT PERKINS

OF

OROOMIAH, PERSIA.

"THE FLOWER FADETH." Isaiah 40: 7.

BOSTON:
JOHN P. JEWETT AND COMPANY.
CLEVELAND, OHIO:
JEWETT, PROCTOR AND WORTHINGTON.
LONDON: LOW AND COMPANY.
1853.

CAMBRIDGE:
ALLEN AND FARNHAM, PRINTERS,
REMINGTON STREET.

PREFACE.

The young stranger, to whom the kind reader is introduced in this brief Memoir, will, it is humbly believed, awaken more than a passing interest, both from the many natural and acquired traits of loveliness which she possessed, and from the circumstances of her birth and residence, as well as her sudden and sorely lamented death, in a far off missionary land.

The beautiful "Persian Flower" indeed soon faded; but it was spared long enough, not only to shed a sweet and lasting fragrance upon the dear circle of missionary and numerous other friends among whom it was graciously permitted to blossom, but also to unfold those richer beauties, which shall bloom, we trust, in immortal verdure, on the "banks of the river of life."

That little Judith, as she will often be designated, (though at her death, she had nearly attained the stature and maturity of womanhood,) was, in the strongest sense, a very remarkable character, will not be urged. Nor is it believed, that the light of her youthful example and loveliness would have been in any sense more sacred and valuable, had she possessed more precocious and unattainable endowments. But that she was a highly gifted and very amiable, as well as dearly beloved, child, will, I think, abundantly appear from the following narrative. Indeed, as is there suggested, Judith was rather remarkable for the beauty and symmetry of her entire character, than for the striking development of any one trait, or any dazzling peculiarity.

And as this fair "flower" may have owed something of its sweetness to the mild and sunny skies of the balmy East, which gave it existence — a land to which the lines of Bishop Heber would not be unaptly applied,

> "Where every prospect pleases,
> And only man is vile,"

so will its loss, from the family and peculiar circle, from which it was so suddenly snatched away, awaken a deeper and more melancholy interest. Under any circumstances, we deeply mourn the premature "nippings of those bright blossoms;" but the heart can but be touched with a more tender sorrow, when the breach is made in the family and circle of missionaries, exiled from the society and congenialities of home and kindred, and subject to the vicissitudes and trials of a residence among a foreign people and in a distant clime.

And as none have perhaps been more fondly cherished, than the few cultivated, exemplary, and pious children of missionaries, who have been providentially allowed to share the fellowship and hospitalities of the churches, so no class, it is believed, will be counted more deserving of prayerful regard and of sacred remembrance, than these precious exotics, reared as they are, amid the corruptions of surrounding ungodliness and depravity. And it is in no small degree with the hope of contributing to a better acquaintance, and a more lively sympathy with these dear offspring of the servants of the churches, that this sketch, interesting peculiarly, as it will perhaps be, to the circle of missionary acquaintances and the numerous friends of our beloved and deeply stricken brother and sister, so often previously bereaved, is given to the public.

There is another consideration, which will give peculiar interest to the following sketch. It is *the memoir of a missionary child;* and as such, gives a glimpse into the interior of missionary life. The family hearth, the private and social endearments, and the every day pursuits and concerns of the missionary's *home*, with which there is a strong and almost universal desire to become acquainted, are here presented, as they cannot well be in the records of general missionary labors, as they appear in our periodicals; or in the memoirs of the more public services of adult missionaries.

It is believed, also, that the numerous notes of condolence, addressed to the bereaved parents, which are introduced towards the close of the volume, will be read with deep interest, as illustrating, in an incidental but affecting manner, the fraternal relations and fellowship existing among missionaries of the same and of different missions.

It is proper to add, what will doubtless occur to those familiar with the productions of the respected father of the deceased, that a large proportion of the matter has been prepared by him. The labor of the writer of this preface has been trifling indeed; and he would only remark in conclusion, that whatever aid he may have furnished, has been most heartily and spontaneously given, as he cannot doubt will also be, the tribute of interest and sympathy felt by the kind reader.

It only remains that we briefly state the history of the larger portrait which accompanies this memoir. The parents had no likeness of the dear child at the time of her death, the rude state of the fine arts, in the land of their missionary sojourn, rendering it difficult to obtain such mementos. In their anguish, after the death of their greatly beloved daughter, with not even the solace of a likeness of her, one of their associates applied to H. A. Churchill, Esq., a very talented young Englishman, who had visited Judith's home about a month before her death, as secretary of the British Commission, under Colonel Williams, for settling the boundary between Turkey and Persia; who was known to be a remarkably skilful artist, and was now at Constantinople, thirteen hundred miles distant from Oroomiah. Four months had elapsed, after Mr. Churchill's very brief acquaintance with Judith, when the application that he should attempt to furnish a likeness of her, reached him. Notwithstanding the difficulties of the undertaking, he kindly and promptly applied himself to the task; how modestly, his own language in the letter accompanying the likeness may best tell: "I have tried to bring together my faint ideas of poor Miss Judith's features, and I herewith forward to you a sketch, which, according to the members of the two commissions, [the British and the Russian,] looks very much like the poor girl. You conceive that it is a very difficult thing; and if you, who have seen more of her, find that the sketch does not in reality resemble her, you will naturally excuse me."

While the portrait, taken under such peculiar disadvantages, bore a strong general resemblance to the original, it had some points of dissimilarity, more easily detected, of course, from recollection, by those long and familiarly acquainted with Judith, than by a stranger. In these circumstances, Mr. Stoddard, one of her parents' associates, applied his skilful hand, (before unpractised on portraits,) and made some slight modifications in Mr. Churchill's picture, the result of which was so successful, that even the Nestorians, who were acquainted with Judith, would instantly weep when that picture met their eyes, though uninformed that it was intended as the portrait of the loved departed one, except by the likeness itself.

A Missionary Associate of Judith's Parents.

Oroomiah, Persia, Jan. 1853.

CONTENTS.

CHAPTER IV.

APTNESS, TACT, AND CAPABILITY.

CHAPTER V.

HER CORRESPONDENCE.

CHAPTER VI.

HER SOCIAL CHARACTER.

CHAPTER VII.

RELIGIOUS INFLUENCES, AND INTEREST.

CHAPTER VIII.

JUDITH'S LAST JOURNEY.

CHAPTER IX.

PROGRESS OF THE DISEASE, AND DEATH.

CHAPTER X.

RETURN AND FUNERAL.

CHAPTER XI.

A DESOLATE HOME.

CHAPTER XII.

NOTES OF CONDOLENCE.

CHAPTER XIII.

NOTES OF CONDOLENCE CONTINUED.

CHAPTER XIV.

CONCLUSION.

MEMOIR.

CHAPTER I.

INFANCY, AND VISIT TO AMERICA.

JUDITH GRANT PERKINS, the subject of this memoir, was a very lovely Persian flower. She was the daughter and fourth child of Rev. J. Perkins, D. D., and Mrs. C. B. Perkins, the first missionaries to the Nestorian Christians, and was born at Oroomiah, Persia, August 8th, 1840. She united in her name the name of her revered paternal grandmother and that of Mrs. Grant, of precious memory, who died at Oroomiah one year and a half before her birth.

About four years before her death, a plate from that grandmother's coffin was sent to her missionary son in Persia, bearing this inscription, — "Judith Perkins, died January 5th, 1848, aged 78;" and under it were three beautiful stanzas from the sweet and gifted pen of Mrs. Sigourney, in her handwriting, and with her signature; also a lock of the departed pilgrim's hair. These tenderly interesting mementoes were sent in a neat frame, which was hung in the parlor of little Judith's home, where it still hangs, and where her eye often rested fondly and thoughtfully upon it.

As a passing notice of that very excellent grandmother, and introductory to the record of the child who bore her name and shared her affection, we here introduce those three stanzas just as they were forwarded.

ON THE DEATH OF MRS JUDITH PERKINS.

"The pilgrim's path was long and lone,
And snows were o'er her temples strown,
Yet still, with courage, firm and high,
And meekness in her heaven-raised eye,
Her course she kept, unmarked by fear,
The thought of home, her soul to cheer,
That promis'd home, among the blest,
Where all the weary hearted rest.

"Though seeds of hallow'd love were sown,
Along the pathway now so lone,
And tendrils from their roots had sprung,
That closely round her bosom clung,
Content to break those cherish'd ties,
And listening for the call to rise,
She oft inquir'd with prayerful sigh,
'How far from home, Oh Lord, am I?'

"Life's last faint steps were travel-wore,
And pangs of sharp disease she bore,
For night and day, with tyrant chain,
The spoiler made each breath a pain;
But on the sky, as earth withdrew,
Her home's fair turrets brighter grew,
While faith the lingering strife sustain'd,
Until its glorious gate she gain'd."

Little Judith was the only "tendril" from Persian soil which that grand parent was ever permitted to behold on earth. Several others in that far-off land had been nipped in the bud by the chills of death, and transplanted to the celestial paradise. But with the most yearning tenderness did the aged saint often embrace this one, as if in the concentration of her love for them all, during a short portion of the little stranger's sojourn in America; and most devoutly did she often implore for that tenderly beloved grandchild the blessings of a covenant-keeping God.

We have called Judith a very lovely Persian flower. She was such, emphatically, throughout her short life. The kind missionary sister,* who first dressed the infant, struck with her peculiar loveliness and sweet quiet, with a fond kiss, said at that time, "She means that we shall all love her;" a remark as prophetic of her

* Mrs. J. Stocking.

subsequent life and character, as it was descriptive of her appearance on the day of her birth.

She was a remarkably quiet child during the period of her infancy; yet happy, active, and playful, to an extent equally remarkable, greatly interesting all who saw her, whether of the members and families of the mission, or of the Nestorians.

Little Judith had not completed one year of her life, when the seriously impaired health of her mother compelled her parents to leave their home and their work, and seek a change, by a visit to America. Brief records of the infant's journey and voyage are found in the volume, published by her father, during that visit, entitled "A Residence of Eight Years in Persia." Of the land journey, he says, "there was a humble individual in our travelling company, whom I have not yet formally introduced, and to whom, as well as to the reader, I perhaps owe an apology. Little Judith, our only surviving child, was eleven months old, when we left Oroomiah. She rode in a pannier, or deep basket, suspended by the side of a horse, and balanced by one of a similar form and dimensions, on the opposite side. In the latter, we carried a few light articles, which we needed during our ride, and which were thus readily accessible. No additional horse was required for the infant, as our servant rode upon the same to keep the baskets adjusted to the pack-saddle. The one in which the child rode was partially lined with a wool cushion, and had a seat of the same fixed near the bottom, with a stick across in front to confine her in her place, while it allowed her to recline sufficiently to sleep. She sometimes remonstrated against being taken from her warm bed, early in the morning, and shut up in her moving prison; but she would soon become quiet, and usually fall asleep, as we moved on, being lulled by the gentle motion of the horse and the music of the bells; or, if these did not suffice, by the shrill lullaby of the kind Nestorian servant. In a few instances the horse fell, with his precious charge half under him; but providentially the child was unharmed and unfrightened, and with the rest of us safely survived the journey, though performed amid the famine, pestilence, and sword." *

This extract sufficiently illustrates the manner in which the infant traveller performed the journey of between six and seven hundred miles, over the rugged and sublime mountains of ancient Pontus and Armenia. Wherever her parents met friends, few and far between, on that long and lonely journey, their infant daugh-

* Residence of Eight Years in Persia, page 477.

ter was an object of attention and admiration. A gentleman* at Erzroom, who had kindly entertained those missionaries a few weeks on their first adventurous journey to Persia many years before, when he was the only civilized resident in that remote Turkish town, now met the mother for the first time after that acquaintance; and at the sight of her, so changed from the bloom of youth and health, to the wan, emaciated appearance of a feeble invalid, his mind suddenly filled with the recollection of her manifold sicknesses, sufferings, and bereavements, during the intervening period, which deeply affected him; yet at that tender moment, as his eye rested on her infant, he could not help remarking, "you have a very fine child there." And the solitary missionary sister,† then residing at Erzroom, in the fulness of her joy in welcoming the parents, on their arrival, in like manner could not suppress the exclamation, as little Judith met her gaze, "Why! have all the children you have lost been as lovely and interesting as this one?" Such expressions were painfully interesting to her parents, raising in their minds the apprehension that the lovely flower might soon be transplanted, as all their other children had been, to a more congenial clime.

* P. Zohrab, Esq. † Mrs. Jackson.

The record of little Judith's voyage to America is thus given in the "Residence of Eight Years in Persia," from which we have above quoted the notice of her land journey. "While this change from the tedium and perils of our long voyage to the freedom of the shore, the greeting of friends after our long absence, and the tender delights of reaching America, were grateful to us beyond description, I must except one of our number. Judith, who was thirteen months old when we left Smyrna, earned an eulogium on the ocean as well as on the land, having thrived wonderfully during the whole of our long rough passage, [of one hundred and nine days,] and seeming to enjoy life at sea far more than anywhere else. She began to walk the day we embarked, and soon became able to run about the deck with a nimbleness that put to blush her fellow passengers, and almost vied with the practised sailors; and she became so fond of the deck, that we found it extremely difficult to quiet her in the cabin during her waking hours, and were obliged to allow her a free range above, even when the vessel was lying to in gales, if it did not actually storm. Without any milk on the passage, and living only on ordinary passengers' fare, she grew rapidly, and was contented and happy to the last, to an extent that astonished all on board." *

It may be added that the infant was *weaned* without milk, and with the least conceivable trouble, during the early part of the passage. Her ceaseless activity and playfulness soon won the heart of the kind and social captain,† who made her his little companion much of the time. In his plain, sailor style, he one day said, playfully, to the parents, "*Judy* ought to be a *boy*, and then she would rough it to some purpose, and traverse the whole world."

The sudden transfer, on reaching New York, from the long and irksome imprisonment on shipboard to an elegant parlor of a hotel, so welcome to the parents, was at last pathetically deplored by the infant voyager, who, taking her stand in the centre of the room, and surveying in turn each strange and imposing object around her, at length met her own little form in the great mirror, and burst into audible weeping.

But little Judith soon found too many kind friends in America, even among strangers, to allow her long to pine for sea life. It would detain us too long to attempt to mention all or a tithe of the acquaintances which she soon

* Residence of Eight Years in Persia, page 491.

† Captain Haven, of Philadelphia.

made, or the attachments she soon formed among those she had never before seen; or to recount the tender kindness which she, as well as her parents, experienced at their hands. She soon won a large place in the hearts of all her relatives who saw her, the survivors among whom, we doubt not, bitterly wept, when the tidings of her early death reached them.

She spent most of the time, during her thirteen months' sojourn in America, in company with her mother, with her maternal grand parents, in Middlebury, Vermont. To those grand parents, she became very tenderly attached; and of her grandpapa, in particular, the late excellent Dr. William Bass, who found more time than other members of the family to caress and play with her, she seemed ever to retain a remembrance, though but two and a half years old when she left him. Often riding on his shoulder to the cupboard, to take a piece of sugar from the bowl with her own tiny fingers, was one of the incidents which she ever afterward associated with him. That fond grandpapa must also have little Judith sit by his side, on her low cricket, while the Bible was read at family worship, and kneel by him, when he carried the family fervently and devoutly to the throne of grace. Often did his speaking eye glance upon the little one, as she thus sat by his side, and most earnestly did he commend her to Israel's Shepherd, at the mercy seat. Her serious, attentive demeanor, at worship, even then, deeply interested and impressed him, and sometimes prompted from him a remark in regard to it. Her father once replied to such a remark, "I am very glad, sir, that you find so much to interest you, in our little daughter." "O, I think she is a remarkable child," rejoined the venerable man, his voice choking, and the tears trickling down his cheeks. "Children's children are the crown of old men; and the glory of children are their fathers."

CHAPTER II.

JUDITH'S RETURN TO PERSIA.

It was with tenderest fondness and many tears, that her numerous relatives and other friends pressed little Judith, for the last time, to their bosoms, and gave her the last kiss, on the eve of her return to Persia. Those parting scenes made a strong impression on the little one. But the inquiry had sometimes come from Persia, during that year, to her parents, from their beloved associates in the field, "When shall we see little Judith's sweet face again?" She had also been told of a playmate, about her own age, far beyond the ocean, who longed to welcome her to her Eastern birthplace; and her little heart thus became interested and *set on going to that distant home.* To the oft repeated inquiry, both in America and on the way, "Where are you going, Judith?" she accordingly replied, "I am going to Persia, to see Waller Holladay." It was with pleasure, therefore, and without one painful regret, that she now parted with friends in the land of her kindred.

Her appearance was peculiarly interesting, when she reëmbarked. It is thus touchingly described by Miss Fisk, in writing to a kind friend* of Judith, soon after her death. "God has taken from us one, who first met my eye, having her little hand held by yours, and being blessed by your kind heart. This was more than nine years ago, and when a frail bark was about to be loosed from its moorings, and to bear a lonely band of missionaries to far off Persia. The little one you so fondly pressed to your bosom on that dreary March day had not then seen three summer's suns. The first short year of her life was passed beneath Persia's lovely skies; and then she was borne to our father-land, to bloom there for a short time, and to win the love of grand parents, uncles, aunts, and cousins, and hundreds more. But when you gave her that fond parting blessing, her young heart was turned to her eastern home; and I remember with what delight she pointed you to the land where her earliest playmate dwelt, and said she would soon be there. Not the mother, with restored health, nor the father, with his faithful message to the churches given, now returning to their loved, chosen home; nor we, who for the first time turned our faces to this

* Mrs. William Reed of Marblehead, Mass.

fair land, were more happy to feel that the winds and the waves were bearing us on their way, than was this little one, whose voyage of life is now ended."

Little Judith contributed much to the life and enjoyment of each passing day among all on board, during the monotony of the voyage to Smyrna. The large company embraced, besides her parents, Mr. and Mrs. Stoddard, Mr. and Mrs. E. E. Bliss, (of Trebizond,) Miss Myers, (now Mrs. Wright,) Miss Fisk, and Mar Yohannan. She was now interested in almost every thing that interested the missionary passengers. If they, at the hour of sunset, or any other time, looked abroad upon the face of the mighty deep, musing in silence on its vastness — the apt emblem of eternity — or in social relaxation watched near their vessel for *fishes*, she too must be lifted up for the same purpose, and never tired of the employment.

When they, to pass usefully the hours of the day, read together in the cabin or on deck, she must be with them, if not to listen to the reading, at least to scan the pictures in some of the books thus read. Her particular favorite was *Hitchcock's Geology*, which was one of the books read in course by the party, and to which she became so much attached, that she was at length inclined to appropriate it as *her book*, hardly being able to loan it to others long enough for the hour's daily reading. It is of course not wonderful for a child to *admire pictures;* but the attachment of little Judith to that book was very peculiar and striking to those who observed it; and the names and forms of some of the minerals described in it, becoming thus familiar to her, made so strong an impression on her mind, that collecting stones, about her home, for her papa's cabinet, on reaching Persia, was one of her earliest and most agreeable pastimes. Often did she enter his study with her little apron stored with pebbles, and with the inquiry, "papa, are not these nice stones?"

So also, when the missionaries raised the spy-glass, to view the distant passing ship, or survey the strange shores which they approached, she too must ever take her turn, in looking at the same objects. And not the smiling Azore islands — the first outlines of sable Africa, or Old Spain — the towering rock of Gibraltar, or its sister pillar of Hercules — the smoke of burning Etna — nor a single cape or island of classic Greece, was oftener or more eagerly, (though of course more intelligently,) gazed upon by them, than by this infant voyager.

On reaching Smyrna, as the anchor struck the bottom of the harbor, Judith, still only a little more than two and a half years old, leaped up from the deck and clapped her little hands, so lively was her sympathy with her parents and the other missionary passengers, in their joy that they had reached *Asia*, and so fully alive was she, to whatever interested them.

She slept with Miss Fisk during the voyage. This kind friend took particular care of Judith, in the feeble health of her mother, both on the ocean and on the land journey; and how little burdensome or irksome to her was the charge, may be inferred from her statement, that the child waked her but in one instance, during the whole rough passage. In this early acquaintance with Miss Fisk, Judith contracted an attachment and regard for her, which she ever afterward ardently cherished, and which exerted much influence on her character. A trifling incident which then occurred, will illustrate the strength of that attachment, as well as the grateful disposition of the child. Observing a small mole on Miss Fisk's face, in her strong desire to be "like aunt Fidelia" in all things, she requested, and repeatedly importuned, that a "spot," as she called it, might be made on her own face, and tried various little expedients to produce one herself.

We may not linger at the different mission stations on the way, and enter with little Judith into the joys of the new acquaintances, which she made at each stopping place, or the reminiscences cherished of her there; but must hasten onward to her Persian home.

The swift steamer bore the missionary band more quickly than "the wings of the wind" from Smyrna to Constantinople. And the matchless splendors of the great city of Constantine, as viewed in approaching it from the sea of Marmora and on entering the spacious harbor — its lofty minarets — massive and shining mosques — gilded palaces — and innumerable other imposing objects, found so interested an admirer in Judith, who pronounced them all *churches*, that not the early hour, nor the inclement air of the bleak morning of their arrival, could confine her in the cabin, after the passengers began to sally forth, at early dawn, for observation.

On board another swift steamer, after a stay of three weeks at the Turkish capital, the missionary party glided up the smiling Bosphorus, and over the frowning Euxine, to Trebizond, where the little traveller's pannier, or deep basket, had found a safe keeping during her visit to America, with the good missionary then residing there, Mr. Johnston; and there she resumed her seat in it, for the long land journey.

She was by no means an uninterested observer on the land, as the missionary pilgrims traversed the sublime mountains, the beautiful valleys, and the vast plains — crossed the ancient river Araxes, and the more venerable Euphrates, or encamped hard by the base of Mount Ararat, on their way to Persia. The frequent and almost interminable caravans, moving in file, with measured step and jingling bells, which they met on the road, also afforded high entertainment for Judith. When inclined, she would sleep as she rode, so that, on halting, unlike the rest of the company, dismounting from their saddles, often much fatigued at the close of a ride of thirty or forty miles, she was never tired, and would run and play about the tent during the remainder of the day.

Arrived, at last, at her long sought *Persian home*, little Judith seemed to share fully with the rest, in the general feelings of joy and thanksgiving. Instead of resuming their residence in the city of Oroomiah, her birthplace, her parents now removed to the health-retreat of the mission, on account of the still feeble health of the mother. This health-retreat is situated six miles south by west of the city, on a gentle declivity of Mount Seir, at a Nestorian village of the same name, which, in Persian, signifies *mount recreation.* It is thus designated, on account of the agreeable attractions which it presents to vast numbers who resort to it for that purpose, from the city and villages below, particularly in the season of spring. This retreat is about a thousand feet above the city and plain; but the ascent to it is so gradual, that it is very easily and pleasantly accessible.

The air is very salubrious on this mountain declivity; and a large spring of fine water, which bursts from the ground just above the mission premises, contributes to the healthfulness of that residence hardly less than the pure air itself. Magnificent views of splendid natural scenery stretch from it to the distance of fifty, seventy, and a hundred or more miles, in all directions, except on the west, where the beautiful grassy Mount Seir, an isolated spur of the lofty Koordish ranges farther back, towers majestically, yet very gracefully, about two thousand feet still above the mission premises, and three thousand above the level of the plain.

At this delightful health residence, the department of translation and other labors in preparing matter for the press of the mission, is principally conducted by Judith's father, though the printing itself is done in the city, under the supervision of Mr. Breath. Here, too, the Nestorian male seminary is situated, which is under the care of Messrs. Stoddard and Cochran, who also reside at Seir. And hither the families of the mission, living in the city, often resort temporarily, especially in the heat and sickliness of summer, for the preservation of their health, or its restoration when impaired. This was *Judith's Persian home.*

Being the tallest and the eldest but one, at the time of her return to Persia, of the juvenile band in the mission, she immediately led the van in their play. She soon ardently loved all those children, and her affection was ever warmly reciprocated by them. As she grew older, she would exercise an almost maternal care over the smaller ones, treating them with the utmost tenderness, and seeming to feel that they were her peculiar charge. She was always delighted with the privilege of assisting their mammas, in taking care of them at their homes, and her ability, as well as her readiness to do this, is seldom equalled in one of her years.

Her attachment to the missionary children was enduring as well as ardent. Her grief was almost inconsolable, when, several years after her return to Persia, she heard of the death of the first Mrs. Stoddard, who died of cholera, at Trebizond, in 1848, not only in her deep sense of the loss sustained by all the mission, in the removal of that estimable friend, but because, as she said, she should "never again see little Harriet and Sarah." She lived to welcome Harriet back to Oroomiah, with a joy long and fondly anticipated, and stronger than can well be conceived; but by an inscrutable providence, as we shall at length see, she was never more permitted to greet little Sarah, (whom she had known only as an infant,) though in the most lively expectation of enjoying that pleasure in the course of a very few days, being on her way to meet her when she died.

CHAPTER III.

HER EDUCATION, AND READING.

JUDITH commenced learning the alphabet, with her loved grandpapa in America, who, it hardly need be stated, took great delight in teaching her, as she would run to him with the separate letters on small cards, when called for by name.

During the first year after her return to Persia, Miss Myers, (now Mrs. Wright,) resided with her parents, and the little one slept with her. Her affectionate heart soon clung fondly to that kind friend, who assisted her mamma in teaching her, in beginning to read and spell. Her aptness in imitating, and her strong desire to emulate those whom she loved, appeared often in this connection, in her care to *sleep straight*, that she might be as tall as "aunt Kate." And it is perhaps not too much to suppose, that something of the remarkably erect and graceful form which marked her growth, may be owing to her childish efforts, at that time, to attain the height of one whom she so much admired.

At an early period, Judith became exceedingly

interested in listening to Scripture narratives, and equally so in reading the Bible, when she became able herself to read. There being no school for the children of the mission, her education naturally devolved on her mamma, who faithfully instructed her in her various studies, and especially in the Holy Scriptures, in which employment both daughter and mother found unspeakable pleasure. The Bible was a book of absorbing interest to her, and she seldom tired of studying it.

She early manifested much tender religious interest, in connection with the study of the Scriptures. She has been known to weep, long and convulsively, in reading the narrative of Christ's betrayal and crucifixion, and she could hardly be quieted on such occasions.

Judith was more or less interested — in some instances very deeply so — in each successive revival among the Nestorians, the first of which occurred when she was only six years old. And her interest was much increased, in one case, by the death of a little brother, and in another case, by the death of a little sister, which occurred in seasons of revival. Two of her notes, to her kind friend, Miss Fisk, written when she was eight years old, and among her earliest attempts at correspondence, are here introduced, as referring to the death of that little sister.

"*Thursday, Jan. 25th,* 1849.

"My dear Miss Fisk,—The Lord has indeed come very near to us, in taking our darling sister. We all loved her very much; but the Lord has seen it best to take her to himself.

"Please give my mother's love, and my own, to Mrs. Stocking, and Miss Rice, and the children.

"Your affectionate friend,

"Judith."

"My dear Miss Fisk,—You asked me to write you again, and so I now write. I was very glad to receive your kind note of Saturday evening. It is true that I loved sister Fidelia most dearly, but I hope that I did not love her too much. You inquired, if I love the Saviour, and hate sin. I hope I do; but we ought not to have false hopes about such things as these.

"My dear mother, and brother Henry Martyn, and myself, all send love to Mrs. Stocking, Miss Rice, and the children.

"Your affectionate friend,

"Judith."

To this last note, Judith's mother added the following postscript:

"My dear Miss Fisk,—Judith wishes mamma to add a postscript to the note, which she has written you to-day. Poor Judith; she seems to be in deep waters about her soul. She says, "O how I wish I could see Miss Fisk, to-night!" I tell her, the work must be with her and God alone; that she must repent of all her sins and give herself to the Saviour. She seems much cast down, and is, I think, under strong conviction of sin. You will all remember this dear child in your prayers. I hope she may now seek in earnest the salvation of her soul.

"Yours truly,

"C. B. P."

Judith often prayed with the pious old Nestorian nurse, who lived in the family, and with other Nestorian females, with deep fervor, particularly in seasons of revival; and she was frequently found instructing and exhorting them on the subject of their salvation. She was from infancy a prayerful child, though much more so in seasons of special religious interest than at other times. Writing to a missionary sister, in regard to another one who was dangerously ill, when the child was three and a half years old, her mother says, "little Judith prays to God, every day, with her mamma, that He 'would make *dear aunt Stoddard* well again, and that little Harriet may not be left without any mamma to take care of her.'" She was accustomed, from early childhood, to lead in prayer by her mother's side, every morning and evening. Though she was ordinarily one of the most lively and playful of children, there was still always a deep religious vein in her feelings, which increased with her age. For several years, she often took her little brother, Henry Martyn, away to pray with her, and other children of the mission occasionally, as she had opportunity. Soon after her death, Henry one day artlessly said, "Judith often used to tell me about Jesus Christ's dying on the cross for sinners, and try to make me understand it, when I was a very little boy."

Judith's eagerness for knowledge, from her earliest childhood, was remarkable. Though the Bible was unspeakably interesting to her, and the book of books in her estimation, it was by no means the only book which she early loved to read. No penalty was so severe to her, as to be required, for any reason, to abstain from reading. And probably few children of her years have read so many books, or retained so much of what they read, as this missionary child. She not only devoured all the small books, as "Peep of Day," "Line upon Line," etc. and juvenile biographies, as "Nathan Dickerman," "Mary Lothrop," and scores of others, that she could find, but she would also eagerly grapple with large books, as the two quarto volumes of the History of Missions, by Choules — Bingham's Sandwich Islands, Layard's Nineveh and its Remains, Lynch's Expedition to the Jordan and the Dead Sea, and many others of similar size, when she was only nine or ten years old. A member of the mission has the impression, that she read Mr. Bingham's volume of more than six hundred large octavo pages — reading it only as a pastime — in twelve or fifteen days. He then questioned her in regard to it, and found her familiar with its contents. Her parents remarked, at the time, that their esteemed friend's book could not have had more hearty admirers in America, than it had in little Judith.

Most of the numerous periodicals, sent to the station, found in her, for several years before her death, as constant and interested a reader, as in any adult member of the mission. With the patriotism and eloquence of Kossuth — the fugitive slave law — the usurpation of the "Prince President," and other passing topics of the day, she was as familiar as most of her seniors.

Her memory was so retentive, that she seldom forgot what she read. She could quote the Bible with great fluency and correctness, and readily give an outline of other books, which she had perused. She had thus always an appropriate anecdote, or illustration, from her reading, for almost every subject introduced at table or elsewhere.

Growing up in the venerable land of the "Medes and Persians," whose customs, like their ancient laws, "change not," and where almost every incident, and indeed almost the entire routine of every day life, is a fresh and luminous exposition of the Bible, she early contracted the habit of minutely observing these vivid illustrations of Scripture scenes and allusions, and took great pleasure in tracing them out, even in her play. A short time before her death, for instance, at a moment of recreation with a playmate, she placed a small stone upon another, and seated on either side, they turned it in the manner of "two women grinding" at the oriental hand mill. A lady who had just joined the mission, happening to observe them, and Judith thinking that she did not comprehend the play, instantly said, in explanation, "two women shall be grinding at the mill; the one shall be taken and the other left." The incident saddened the missionary sister at the time, naturally suggesting, that one of the two dear children might ere long "be taken," an apprehension very soon to be sorrowfully realized.

While Judith's general interest in reading, and in the acquisition of knowledge, was such as we have stated, there were particular books which she read, that made a peculiarly deep and lasting impression on her mind and heart. One such book was the Memoir of Mary Lothrop, which her mother read to her before she could herself read, though she must stand at her elbow, hold the book with one hand, and point to the line with a finger of the other.

Another book which very deeply and more permanently affected her, was the Memoir of Margaret Davidson, which she read with her mother when about nine years old. As some of the readers of this biography may not be familiar with that memoir, and as it made so strong and enduring an impression on Judith, we here introduce a brief notice of the subject of it, from the graphic and truthful pen of the lamented Prof. B. B. Edwards, D. D. "On the 25th November, 1838, a young lady died at Ballstown, in the State of New York, in the sixteenth year of her age. She seemed hardly to be a creature of earth, but to have wandered here by accident, from some more blessed region than ours. There were about her a grace, a strange purity — a sunny brightness — which were not so much *genius*, as mind in its *freed* state. We have never heard or read of one of human mould, who was more perfectly divested of the grossness which appertains to our condition here. Yet she possessed all the innocent feelings of humanity. Never did one pass a blither childhood. She had not a particle of that acid melancholy which is sometimes allied to genius.

"The first sentence which breaks from the lips of the unreflecting reader, on rising from the contemplation of her brief career, is, that such a gift is not to be coveted. We should shrink from having ought to do with one so etherial. We look with fear and trembling on a flower which shows its delicate petal in February. Give us the hardy plant that can endure the early frost and summer heat. Intrust us with the intellect which has some alliance with earth, — some fitness to its stern necessities.

"Others in perusing this volume, [the memoir of Margaret,] will give us a homily on the imprudence of parents and teachers. Her premature death, they say, is a warning which should not be neglected. It shows the imminent hazard of stimulating the susceptible faculties to an intemperate and fatal growth.

> 'But we are glad she lived thus long,
> And glad that she has gone to rest.'

Her course was ordered in perfect wisdom. May she not have done that which the longest career of usefulness, as it is commonly termed, fails to do? May she not have had a sublimer errand than others have? May not her brief sojourn throw some light on the mystery of our nature? We gain a vivid idea of a human soul. The thick veil is for a moment lifted up. She had the light and airy movement of a winged spirit. We seem to be gazing on the delicate structure of a seraph; and yet she had the yearning sympathy of a child of earth." *

It is not strange that the memoir of such a young lady, by the pen of Washington Irving, from materials furnished by the gifted mother, should have taken a strong hold on the interest and feelings of one possessing the mind and temperament of little Judith. We would not compare the cast or compass of her intellect with that of the soaring, ethereal Margaret Davidson; but it was fully competent to feel the transcendent power and charms of the character of that rare mortal, even through the medium of a memoir. Particularly did Judith's sympathies flow forth with hers, in her ardent admiration of the beauties and sublimities of nature. This missionary child was eminently a child of nature, which appeared in her every motion. If she walked abroad, over the hills around her home, she *must* always *run and leap*, in unison with the sporting lambs, or gurgling cascades. She must

* Address delivered at the fourth anniversary of the Mount Holyoke Female Seminary, July 29th, 1841.

dip and drink water right from the sparkling fount of the crystal spring; bathe her head in the cool stream below, and "spatter" briskly there with her playmates. She passionately loved to bask in the genial sun, and inhale the pure fresh air, under the open sky, unencumbered by veil, hood, or bonnet. This general love of nature, which was strongly innate in her, was very perceptibly quickened by the perusal of that memoir.

From that time, the starry heavens, so bright and glorious in Persia, presented new attractions to Judith. In this land of ancient "star-gazers," and from the clearness of its atmosphere, of all others naturally the most favorable to the cultivation of the sublime science of astronomy, and where a member * of the Nestorian mission has solved the long disputed problem of Jupiter's moons being visible to the naked eye, she often lingered on the flat roof of her home, sometimes alone, and sometimes with her mother or little brother, till the last glimmering of twilight had long disappeared, fondly surveying "the hosts of heaven," many of which she could call by name; her thoughts most vividly associating with them the majesty and glory of their great creator.

And the vast panorama of beauty, grandeur, and sublimity of the terrestrial scenery, that al-

* Rev. David T. Stoddard.

ways met her eye, from her mountain home,—the city directly below—the great plain beyond, and on either hand, dotted with almost countless verdant and smiling villages—and the placid lake, bounding the plain, and like an extended mirror, reflecting the effulgence of the brilliant Persian sun—and, farther still, the towering ranges of mountains, rising in the blue distance and blending with the sky,—this whole scene, rarely surpassed or equalled in the wide world, now possessed new charms in her view, and she daily gazed on it with unutterable emotions of enjoyment.

From this time, too, she listened with new interest to "the fowls of heaven," "which sing among the branches." In this Eastern land, where all nature is peculiarly instinct with life, and almost every department of it presents a strikingly luxuriant development; the birds are remarkable for the richness and beauty of their plumage, and the fulness and sweetness of their notes. A few species of these winged songsters congregate regularly, in immense numbers, at early morn and at twilight, in the clusters of trees around Judith's home, and most melodiously warble forth their choral matins and vespers, besides more irregular chants at all hours of the day. In her they ever found an enraptured listener and admirer, but particularly after her perusal of the memoir in question.

And from this time, also, her love of *flowers*, which had always been quite strong, was greatly increased. Her little flower-garden was now more carefully cultivated; and the whole mountain around her home — itself in spring like one immense flower-garden, smiling in bright colors and redolent with sweet fragrance, where a thousand hives of bees annually revel and amass their luscious stores — now presented new charms, and more strongly than ever tempted her forth in frequent rambles, for specimens to press for preservation. About this time, she prepared a collection of pressed flowers and sent them to a cousin in America.

Another immediate effect of her reading that memoir, was a quickened taste and relish for poetry, — the portions of Margaret's poetry, contained in the memoir, having deeply interested her. Mrs. Sigourney, who had sent several small volumes of her writings to Judith and her parents, now became her favorite author. She read and re-read those books with her mother, as also other poetry, with most engrossing and ever increasing interest.

One of the last books which Judith read in course — and read aloud to her mother — was "Uncle Tom's Cabin," kindly sent to her father by a friend in America — one of the gentlemanly publishers — a short time before her death. It is certainly not strange, that the whole of that wonderful book broke up the deep fountains of her feeling soul. But *little Eva* was the character in it, which most deeply interested Judith. Indeed, her heart seemed like melted wax, while reading that thrilling sketch, and to receive from it, as from a seal, a full and perfect impression. She longed to be like Eva, and to be with her. And as Providence ordered, it would almost seem, that that seraphic character was presented to her, just at that time, as a beckoning angel, to invite her to her celestial home. The congeniality of Judith's spirit and character with Eva's, was more than imaginary, and obvious to the general observer. Mr. Stevens, British consul in Persia, while reading "Uncle Tom's Cabin," lent to him by Judith's father a short time after her death — and in his own language, reading it "with greater interest and more pain" than he ever read any other book — remarked as follows: "A wonderfully interesting character is that Evangelina. There was a great deal in her that strongly reminds me of poor Judith."

The perusal of that affecting sketch exerted a very salutary influence on Judith's mind, in turning her thoughts vividly toward the subject of death and heaven, as presented in Eva's history. And of all the myriads who have wept over that sketch, few probably have more fully sympathized with the spirit of the following admired stanzas by Whittier, than could the youthful subject of this memoir.

"Dry tears for holy Eva;
With the blessed angels leave her.
Of the form so sweet and fair,
Give to earth the tender care.
For the golden locks of Eva,
Let the sunny south land give her
Flower pillow of repose,
Orange bloom and budding rose.

"All is light and peace with Eva;
There the darkness cometh never;
Tears are wiped and fetters fall,
And the Lord is all in all.
Weep no more for happy Eva;
Wrong and sin no more shall grieve her;
Care and pain and weariness
Lost in love so measureless.

"Gentle Eva — loving Eva —
Child confessor — true believer;
Listener at the Saviour's knee,
'Suffer such to come to me.'
O for faith like thine, sweet Eva;
Lighting all the solemn river,
And the blessing of the poor,
Wafting to the heavenly shore."

CHAPTER IV.

HER APTNESS, AND CAPABILITY.

JUDITH'S education, it should be borne in mind, was conducted by her mother almost entirely *alone*, without any of the incitements of the school-room and class-mates, to awaken and sustain an interest in her studies. Few indeed are the children, who would have progressed as she did, in such circumstances. She was kindly taught, a few weeks, with other children of the mission, by Misses Fisk and Rice, in connection with the Nestorian girls of their seminary; and a few weeks more, in two instances, by Mrs. Coan. With these exceptions, she was instructed *solitarily* by her mamma, until two months before her death. Yet she was never listless in learning or reciting her lessons; but ever engaged in them, with an interest, enthusiasm, and success, which often alike surprised and chided her teacher, who, while the task of instructing her was a very delightful one, was sometimes so much occupied with domestic cares, that she found it difficult to redeem the time which her beloved pupil required and richly deserved.

Judith's aptness and capability in study, were equally conspicuous in other things. When she was ten years old, her father received a *seraphine*, which was sent to him as a present, by a kind friend* in America, to be kept and used in his family, for the special benefit of the male seminary. At her tender age, she soon commenced using the instrument, and with a rapidity that astonished all who witnessed her progress, she became able, in a short time, to play beautifully at religious worship, with fewer hours of instruction from her early friend, Mrs. Wright, than she was herself years old. And many evenings have the forty pupils of the male seminary assembled, in a large room at her home, to sing the songs of Zion, led on by her as by a little seraph, playing charmingly on that sweet instrument. The evenings, thus spent, were seasons of high enjoyment to her, not only as a lover of music, but from the delight which she felt, in imparting gratification and improvement to those young Nestorians, who were to become teachers and preachers among their people.

The twilight of Sabbath evening, which she divided between the instrument and walking on the terrace, was her favorite season for using the seraphine in sacred music. In concert with her

* Luke Sweetser, Esq., of Amherst, Mass.

parents and little brother, several sweet hymns were played and sung by her, at that hallowed hour. Her last piece, on the last Sabbath evening of her life — and indeed the last piece that she ever played — was the following familiar hymn: —

"Jerusalem, my glorious home,
Name ever dear to me;
When shall my labors have an end,
In joy and peace in thee?

"O when, thou city of my God,
Shall I thy courts ascend,
Where congregations ne'er break up,
And sabbaths have no end?

"There happier bowers than Eden's bloom;
No sin nor sorrow know.
Blest seats! through rude and stormy scenes
I onward press to you.

"Why should I shrink at pain or woe?
Or feel at death dismay?
I've Canaan's goodly land in view,
And realms of endless day."

Those were very happy Sabbath hours to Judith, here on earth, but were doubtless the prelude to infinitely happier ones, now enjoyed by her in heaven.

Her proficiency, in learning to play on the seraphine, almost uninstructed, is but an illustration of her tact and success, in accomplishing almost any thing to which she turned her attention, and in which she was interested. During the last spring of her life, Mrs. Stoddard kindly gave her, and some of her playmates, a few lessons in *botany*, to which she had never before attended. She eagerly engaged in this study. It opened a new and delightful range to her thoughts, leading her systematically into new mysteries of nature, (of which, in its various departments, as we have stated, she was a very ardent admirer,) and through nature up to nature's God. Mrs. Stoddard's lessons were daily and minutely repeated by Judith to her mamma, with characteristic accuracy and enthusiasm.

About a year before her death, she read a little book, entitled "Jane Hudson," which awakened in her a desire and an ambition to become a "school teacher," or rather, quickened that desire, which had long existed in her bosom. And she embraced the earliest opportunity, afterward, of a visit of Mrs. Stocking and her children, a few days on Mount Seir, to gather her playmates, several hours a day, in the capacity of a school, her ideas of which she had received from the Nestorian Female Seminary. Day after day, the children assembled and spent a few hours in study and recitation, under Judith's tuition, with perfect order, stillness, and propriety. On the last day of the visit, the parents were invited by her to an *examination.* They attended, and were exceedingly gratified and entertained, by the exhibition of those children — even to declamation by the little boys — for which they had prepared themselves the few previous days, under the superintendence of their juvenile teacher between ten and eleven years old. To the inquiry addressed to her little brother, since her death, "How did Judith keep her scholars in such order?" he replied, "She used to tell them, that, if they were good children, she would pin a certificate of their good behaviour on their shoulders, to wear home."

The modern Syriac language, which Judith spoke with much fluency, she learned to *read* without the assistance of any regular teacher, and apparently almost wholly unaided. Her desire to read "The Rays of Light," the monthly Nestorian periodical, as also to be able to teach Nestorian females, seemed to be the particular motive that prompted her thus to learn to read that language.

Her aptness and maturity were also conspicuous, in the cares of the family. In the feeble health of her mother, she shared largely in those cares, and in some instances, they devolved on Judith for days at a time. In the absence of other help, a few months before her death, she made the bread for the family, several weeks in succession. Her success, in domestic cares and labors, were equalled only by the interest and delight with which she engaged in them.

On this general subject, Mr. Cochran, who resides in the same yard with Judith's parents, bears the following testimony. "Having had daily opportunities, for several years, of observing her womanly desire to make herself useful in every sphere, and having habitually witnessed her untiring and very welcome offices of kindness, in my own family, both by day and by night, in times of sickness,—and her very matronly superintendence of my little children, and fruitful devices to contribute to their amusement and happiness,—her prompt attendance in leading them to the Sabbath school, and her invariable eagerness to accompany them to their home, in adjoining apartments to her own, and to their nursery, to consummate the labors of her self-assumed charge, after an evening meeting or a social interview. I feel that too much can hardly be said, in deserved praise of the skill of her youthful hands, or the benevolence and kindness of her heart."

While studying in connection with the Nestorian Female Seminary, a short time, as already mentioned, Judith was kindly boarded by Mr. and Mrs. Coan, of Gawar, who then resided in the city of Oroomiah. Mr. Coan thus speaks of her, in a letter to her parents, after her death. "We take a melancholy pleasure in recalling the time when Judith was a member of our family at Oroomiah, the few weeks she attended the school of Misses Fisk and Rice. Although then but ten years old, she had a womanly bearing and dignity, which are not often found in those of riper years. Her care for Henry, who took his dinners with us, but went home at night, was truly motherly. Her anxiety lest she should give us trouble, and her desire to render herself useful, showed a thoughtfulness and regard for the comfort of others, of which many would-be-polite know little.

"While with us, she was very diligent in her studies, often begging us to remain up a little longer, evenings, than we thought best for her.

"During our short acquaintance with her at that time, I was surprised and delighted to find her mind, young as she was, stored with so much and so varied reading. But her improvement in mind and manners, and in general intelligence, appeared very striking in my visit to you last spring, after an absence of six months in Gawar; and her quiet, subdued, yet cheerful spirit, her apparent interest and delight in spiritual conversation, and her tenderness and concern for her soul, manifested in a short conversation I then had with her, led me to hope, that grace had begun a good work in her heart, and I trust that her Saviour was even then sanctifying her for himself, and preparing her for the great change which awaited her.

"But why should I dwell on the many pleasing traits of your beloved Judith? You know them all; and yet I may not be deprived of the privilege of expressing to you my condolence, and assuring you that we too loved Judith, and with you feel her loss."

Successful as Judith had been in prosecuting her studies *alone*, under her mother's instruction, with the brief exceptions we have mentioned, it had long been her ardent desire to enjoy the privileges of a *school;* and her young heart leaped with ecstasy, in the definite and near prospect of welcoming a teacher, when she heard that Miss Harris had been designated to instruct the children of the mission, in connection with other missionary labors. The following notes, addressed by Judith to Miss Harris, while on her way to Oroomiah, will show the interest of the child on this subject.

"*Oroomiah, Oct. 16th*, 1851.

"My dear Miss Harris, — I am very happy to have the opportunity of addressing one, whom I hope soon to call, *teacher*. We are all very happy to learn, that we shall so soon *have a teacher*. We once had a little school, taught by Mrs. Coan, in the school-room where we hope to spend so many happy hours with you. Our present teacher is mamma.

"Mamma and papa and brother Henry unite with me in much love to you. Please accept this from your affectionate friend,

"JUDITH G. PERKINS."

The foregoing note reached Miss Harris at Smyrna. The following is her reply to it and to other notes which she received from the children at Oroomiah. It was written, as will be perceived, after her arrival at Constantinople.

"*Constantinople, March* 1*st*, 1852.

"My dear Judith, Harriet, Lucy, Jerusha, William, and all the children of Oroomiah,— Your kind notes of October were received a few days since. You can imagine the joy they gave me, after my long passage. I soon felt that I was almost acquainted with you, and that I should soon feel at home in Oroomiah; for I trust, that before many months, I shall be with you.

"Until I can cross the mountains, I am to remain in Bebek, and teach the children of the families here. They had expected me to have been with them all winter; but my winter has been spent upon the ocean, and I did not arrive at Constantinople until almost spring. But now that I am no longer to be carried forward by wind and tide, I hope there will be no disappointment about my reaching Oroomiah.

" I am not only interested in those who are to be my pupils, but in the account of your schoolroom, etc. I am now teaching in quite a small room, and for this reason, not able to receive several English scholars who wish to come. In Pera and Bebek together, there are now twenty-two missionary children; but it is seldom that they can all be in school at the same time. Mrs. Hinsdale has a very pleasant school in Pera. And before I came here, Mrs. Shauffler taught her four boys, and Miss Lovell the girls in Bebek.

" While I remain here, I shall be happy to hear from you; and when the snow shall have melted from the mountains, I hope to be with you, to receive the welcome you so kindly offer me. Till then, may God bless you and me, and I pray you accept much love,

" From your affectionate friend,

" Martha A. Harris."

The following is a second note from Judith to Miss Harris.

"*Oroomiah*, *April 30th*, 1852.

"MY DEAR MISS HARRIS,—I thank you very much for your kind and welcome note. It seems as though I could hardly realize, that you are at Constantinople, so near us, and that so soon, we are to have the pleasure of welcoming you to our Persian home.

"When I last wrote you, there were but thirteen children in the mission, besides the three who came here to be educated; but now, as Dr. Wright has a little son about three months old, John Henry, there are fourteen, and the other three make seventeen. Only eleven are old enough to go to school.

"Mrs. Stoddard has a class in botany. We think it a very pleasant study. There are some very pretty flowers that grow wild here. We also have a Sabbath school. Mrs. Stoddard is our teacher. We enjoy it very much. We also meet together once in two months, (as we are not able to get together oftener,) for a missionary meeting. Mr. Breath, (who meets with the children at their missionary concert,) is treasurer. We intend to send our money to *Bootan*, and support a missionary there.

"Mamma sends her love to you. Please accept this, with much love,

"From your affectionate young friend,

"JUDITH G. PERKINS."

When Miss Harris approached Oroomiah, Judith's long cherished desire, to go a few days' journey and meet her, was strongly revived, and was gratified by the kindness of Mr. and Mrs. Stoddard, who went to Khoy, to help and cheer that missionary sister over the wearisomeness and loneliness of the way, and took Judith with them.

The children's teacher finally reached her destination, on the 2nd of July, 1852, and Judith's cup of joy seemed full. With unspeakable gratification, she attended the long anticipated school seven weeks, and then her place in it was suddenly vacated forever.

The grief of that teacher, occasioned by the death of her eldest pupil, so soon after she reached the field, — the pupil with whose name her future labors had been intimately associated in her mind, in America, and on her long and weary way to Persia, may be better conceived than described. It is not strange, that she pathetically said, as the tears coursed rapidly down her cheeks, the day after Judith's funeral, "it now seems to me as though my work was done."

But besides her direct labors for the Nestorians, there are many other children in the mission, who, though younger, will, if spared, soon reach Judith's age, and now equally need that teacher's laborious care; and the youngest will erelong swell the number of her precious, important, and responsible charge. She can still aid the feeble and toil-worn missionary mothers, encouraging their hearts and strengthening their hands; and relieve the burdened missionary fathers, enabling them to give themselves more fully "to the ministry of the word," and rendering them more cheerful, contented, and efficient in their labors, than when borne down with care and solicitude for their children, without a school, and may probably thus protract, by many years, the period of their missionary service. She can contribute to rear more sweet "Persian flowers," to bloom and shed forth their blessed fragrance, and aid essentially in the evangelization of this benighted land, as did young Judith, by the grace of God and through her mother's instruction.

But Judith's vacant seat in that school, will never be forgotten, nor unmourned, by either teacher or pupils. They now often give utterance to their feelings of bereavement, by singing, within the saddened walls of their pleasant school-room, which is situated on the terrace, where Judith used daily to walk, and play, and meditate, and admire the "handiworks" of God, the sweet hymn, of which the following stanzas are a part:—

"Death has been here and borne away,
A sister from our side;
Just in the morning of her day,
As young as we, she died.

"We cannot tell who next may fall,
Beneath the chastening rod;
One must be first, but let us all
Prepare to meet our God."

Next to Judith's strong desire for a school at Oroomiah, was her fond anticipation of one day becoming a member of the Mount Holyoke Female Seminary, in America. This was the summit of her aspirations, in regard to her education. She had, for several years, regularly read the journals sent from that seminary to its missionary graduates; and she earnestly longed to enjoy the privileges of that school of revivals, and other good things, from which her kind friends, Miss Fisk, Miss Rice, and Mrs. Stoddard had come, and from which one of her cousins often wrote her, during the last two years of her life, urging her to come to America, and dwell with her kindred. Her perusal of the memoir of Miss Lyon, the illustrious founder of that Seminary, finally gave intense effect to all her previous longings on the subject.

The desire of being ready to enter Mount Holyoke Seminary, at the prescribed age, enhanced her zeal in her studies, even when she was quite small. As illustrating this point, and the interest always taken in her proficiency by Miss Fisk, and especially in her religious welfare, the following note from that friend, acknowledging the *first note*, ever written by Judith, is here inserted.

"*City*, *Oct.* 27*th*, 1848.

"MY DEAR JUDITH, — I was very glad to receive your little note yesterday. I think that you did very well for the first time. I will keep your note, so as to tell you, when you are grown up, how old you were, when you began to write letters. I think that you will be able to write your grandpapa pretty soon. Do you not think that he would be very much pleased to receive a letter from you? I am sure that he would.

"I hope that you love to study as well as write. How many pages have you learned in your arithmetic? Learn as fast as you can, so as to be ready to go to Mount Holyoke when you are sixteen. Perhaps your papa and mamma will read to you about Miss Washburn, who died there last summer. I remember her very well. She was but a little larger than you are now, when I came from America with you and our other good friends. I hope you will love the Saviour as she did.

"Thank little Fidelia and Mary for their kisses, and give them some very sweet ones from aunt Fidelia. My love also to your papa and mamma. I shall always be very glad to hear from you. Much love to yourself from your affectionate friend,

"FIDELIA FISK."

The following is Judith's note above-mentioned, which, as being her *first*, is here inserted.

"*Seir, Oct. 24th*, 1848.

"Dear Miss Fisk, — As you said I might write you letters, I now make my first attempt. We are all very well. Father and mother send love to you. Yours truly,

"Judith."

"P. S. Mary and Fidelia both send love and kisses to aunt Fidelia. J."

As a source of high enjoyment and of health, as well as of improvement, and indicative of her tact and capability, we should not omit to mention Judith's riding on a saddle; there having, until recently, been no wheel carriages in Oroomiah. From the age of five years until ten, she was accustomed to ride on a white donkey, of the kind common in the south of Persia, which was gentle, and easily managed by a child. During the last two years of her life, she rode an equally gentle pony, presented to her by an English gentleman,* which she greatly prized and admired. The friend who presented him to her, died suddenly at Tehrân, a few months before her death.

* Dr. F. Casolani.

Judith was exceedingly fond of riding, in which she soon became very expert, and even heroic. On one long journey, in particular, when but ten years old, in company with her parents and Mr. and Mrs. Coan, she courageously and successfully crossed some of the most rugged and sublime mountain ranges of Koordistan, on her careful donkey. This early exercise on a saddle contributed to impart a vigor and independence to her mind, as well as strength to her body, which hardly any thing else could have done.

The journey with Mr. and Mrs. Stoddard, already mentioned, was performed on her favorite pony; and in no instance did she ever seem to enjoy riding more than on that journey, which she often mentioned afterward, as one of the happiest weeks of her life. The journey on which she died, yet to be described, was performed, and with great enjoyment, on the same gentle animal. As he was led home desolate, after being suddenly bereft of his youthful rider on the road, a member of the mission remarked, "the donor and the owner are now both gone."

CHAPTER V.

CORRESPONDENCE.

It is of course not to be expected, that a child, who died at the age of twelve years, would leave behind her an extensive correspondence, to illustrate her character and attainments. A considerable portion of Judith's notes and letters, and those prepared with the most care, and probably the most interesting, as indicating her religious feelings, are on the other side of the globe, scattered among her relatives and friends,—too far away to be recovered for this purpose. Enough, however, are introduced, to serve as specimens of the ease and maturity of her style. These were always very striking, in her conversation. It is recollected, that a member of the mission, while one day observing her at play with her little brother, when she was five years old, suddenly burst into laughter, assigning as the reason, that he was "so much amused, with the *aged* expressions of that child, even in her play."

Something of the maturity of her language may, indeed, have been owing to her circumstances, early associating mostly with her parents and their fellow laborers, and removed from the general society of children; but not all; for she was peculiar, in this respect, among the missionary children; and her maturity was as marked in the topics and ideas, as in the style, of her conversation.

During the last few months of her life, there was a mission station in *Gawar*, an extensive and beautiful valley, or elevated plain, among the lofty mountains of Koordistan, about seventy miles west of Oroomiah. Mrs. Coan, the only female missionary who resided at that new station, during the first year after it was commenced, kindly numbered Judith among her regular and familiar correspondents, primarily for the gratification and improvement of the child. We now introduce a note from Mrs. Coan; and several follow from Judith to her, in the order of their date, which are interesting not so much of course for the intrinsic importance of their contents, as being the artless, unstudied effusions of her own mind.

"*Gawar, April 12th*, 1852.

"My dear Judith,— My note to you must necessarily be short, as I have but little time, and I cannot write late at night. We rise quite early, half-past five, (though perhaps you in

Oroomiah will not call it early,) and I retire as early as ten.

"I am very glad our letters interest you so much. I am sure it is a great pleasure to us to write, when we have something to communicate, which is not so often as I could wish.

"You seem to have very pleasant times, and to be enjoying yourselves very much, and I am very glad it is so. I hope you are also improving your opportunities for usefulness; for even a little girl like you may be useful in many respects; if in no other, by setting a good example before all whom she meets. Being the eldest of the children, all naturally look to you for a pattern; and I hope it is such as you will not be ashamed of, at some future day.

"You are often reminded that time is short. I suppose that *Iwaz* * little thought he had so few days to live, when he returned to the seminary, after vacation. So we know not the day nor the hour, when we may be called to lie down and die. O let us strive to be ready, whenever it may be!

"Much love to Henry and for yourself. I remain your affectionate friend,

"S. P. Coan."

* A member of the male seminary, who died at Seir.

From Judith to Mrs. Coan.

"*Oroomiah, Dec. 9th*, 1851.

"My dear Mrs. Coan, — As Mr. Stocking and Mr. Stoddard are leaving to-morrow for Gawar, I take the opportunity to write you a short note. We have missed you and your family, (including Mr. Rhea,) very much, since you went to Gawar, especially on thanksgiving day. We children, as usual, counted all that were seated in our parlor, and found four missing. Mr. Stoddard preached the sermon, and Mrs. Stoddard prepared the thanksgiving supper. Three hymns were sung, and I played the tunes on the seraphine. They were Ortonville, Balerma, and Olmutz.

"Henry and myself go on regularly with our studies; I also practise daily on the seraphine, and am learning to sing a little. I led the singing at our last children's monthly concert. I must now close. With sincerest love to Mr. Coan, Mr. Rhea, and Alexander,

"Believe me most truly yours,

"Judith."

"*Oroomiah, Jan. 1st*, 1852.

"My dear Mrs. Coan, — I wish you all a happy new year. As Dr. Wright and Mr. Breath intend visiting Gawar, I take my pen with great pleasure, to answer your kind note. I am very sorry to hear, that you have the face ache, and hope that you will soon get over it. In your note, you ask how many hours a day I practise on the seraphine. I think about an hour and a half. You also ask, what we study. I study Parley's Universal History — Arithmetic — Geography — and Speller and Definer; also Grammar. Henry studies Arithmetic, Geography, Spelling, and Reading. I am very happy to hear that Alexander is getting on so well in his studies.

"We have heard that Miss Harris has left America.

"Mamma sends her love to you. Her head aches, this morning, or she would write you.

"Please give my sincerest love to Mr. Coan, Mr. Rhea, and Alexander, and accept this hastily written note (as I have not time to copy it).

"From your affectionate friend,

"JUDITH G. PERKINS."

"*Oroomiah, Feb. 2d*, 1852.

"DEAR MRS. COAN, — I thank you very much for your kind note, and my only apology for not answering it, by the last messenger, is, that I had no time, being Henry's amanueusis, in writing to Alexander, and it being late in the evening when I commenced.

"To day I read your journal through, and was very glad to know how you pass your days at your mountain home. How much surprised you must have been, to hear that Mr. Breath had come. I was very glad to hear that you could get out at all, even on a hand sled. I hope you enjoyed your ride. While Mr. Breath was gone to Gawar, I stayed with Mrs. Breath. She was rather anxious about him. Papa told her, he hoped that she was not sorry he had gone. She said, 'I shall not be, after he returns.'

"I hope I shall be able to write to Mr. Rhea. Please give my love to him — also to Mr. Coan and Alexander — accepting a large share for yourself.

"From your affectionate friend,

"JUDITH G. PERKINS."

To appreciate some of the allusions in the preceding note, the reader should be informed, that the elevated district of Gawar, hemmed in on all sides by the lofty Koordish mountains, is subject to terrible storms of snow during its long winter. It is significantly called by the natives, "*the snow treasury.*" The entire fall of snow on the plain, during the first winter's residence of the missionaries there, which was pronounced by the Nestorians an uncommonly mild season, was about eighteen feet, there being from seven to nine feet on level, for a considerable period. Hence the difficulty of Mrs. Coan's getting out for exercise.

The high range of mountains, which separates Gawar from Oroomiah, is usually rendered impassable, several months of the year, for any beast of burden; and footmen, who travel with broad moccasins, or on wicker snow-shoes, are often in imminent peril, and sometimes perish, in storms or blows that suddenly overtake them, in crossing that mountain. Dr. Wright accompanied Mr. Breath on his way to Gawar, to the top of that high range, and there turned back, finding the travelling so difficult, that the journey would require a longer period than he could be absent from his family. Mr. Breath proceeded alone, and hence the solicitude respecting him, referred to in the foregoing note.

Mrs. Breath thus speaks of Judith's stay with her, during her husband's absence. "Dear Judith's allusion to her visit with me, in the note of February 2d to Mrs. Coan, calls many tender recollections of her to my mind. She was so womanly—so pleasant a companion! Our evenings were delightfully spent, in reading poetry, which she so highly enjoyed. On Sabbath evening, she proposed reciting such hymns as we could from memory. At my request, hers were sung. It was a happy hour to us both."

"*Oroomiah, Feb. 26th*, 1852.

DEAR MRS. COAN, — I thank you very much for the kind advice your note contained. I esteem it a great favor, that you, with all your labors and cares, should write me, when you have so many other correspondents. I am sorry to hear that you have not been able to ride out on your sled, but am glad you can get out at all.

"Last Friday, we went down to the city in our sleigh. When we went down, it was pretty good going; but in coming up, there was so much bare ground, that papa said, he really thought it was the last sleigh-ride we should take, this winter. Yesterday, we went down to the city and found Caty Wright sick with a high fever.

"Poor Hosmer,* who has long been very ill, lies apparently at the point of death.

"To-morrow, the pupils of the male seminary have a vacation; and after four weeks, the girls will have one.

"Will you be so kind as to give my love to Mr. Rhea. As the messenger goes to-morrow morning, I fear that I shall not have time to acknowledge his note to the children, by this opportunity.

* A pious Nestorian woman, in the village of Seir.

"Please give my love to Mr. Coan and Alexander, accepting much for yourself.

"From your affectionate young friend,

"JUDITH."

It is proper to state, that the vehicle, dignified by the title of *sleigh*, in the above note, would hardly bear that epithet in America. It was a rude sled, constructed by Judith's father, for the double purpose of amusing his children and giving them exercise in winter. Yet, it was the nearest to the sleigh *species*, of any thing they had ever seen.

"*Oroomiah, March 18th*, 1852.

"DEAR MRS. COAN, — The reason I did not answer your other note by the first messenger was, that I was not feeling well at the time. The next Saturday after the messenger left, I was taken sick; on Sunday I had a high fever, all day, and took medicine; on Monday, I sat up a little; on Tuesday, I was some better, but did nothing all that week.

"Perhaps you would like to know how my time is occupied. We usually finish prayers and breakfast, about eight o'clock. From that time till half-past nine, I help mamma. I study from that time till after twelve. From then till two o'clock, I have stepping-about work, dinner, etc.,

etc. From two o'clock till three, I sew or knit. At three, I go on the roof to walk. At four, I sometimes play on the seraphine, or write. At five, we have tea. At six, I play on the seraphine an hour. At seven, mamma reads to us an hour, and I knit. I then read half an hour, and then comes my bed time.

Sabbath * before last was so stormy, that none of the ladies or children came up from the city to meeting; but Mr. Breath thought that the children here had better have their missionary meeting, though there were only five, as we had not had one for two months, and would not, perhaps, be able to get together for some time to come. We sung the 581st hymn [Church Psalmody] beginning with the verse,

'Now in the heat of youthful blood,
Remember your Creator, God;
Before the months come hastening on,
When you shall say, my joys are gone.'

Though we are so few, we raised one *tomon*, two *sahib korans*, and one *shâhi;* [about two dollars and a half].

"Please give my love to Mr. Coan, Mr. Rhea, Sanem, and Alexander.

"From your affectionate friend,

"JUDITH G. PERKINS."

* Being communion Sabbath, when the mission are usually all together.

" *Oroomiah, April 3d*, 1852.

" Dear Mrs. Coan, — Yesterday afternoon papa came down stairs, saying the Gawar mail had come; and each one asked, 'have I got a letter?' Henry was reciting his lesson in arithmetic, and was very impatient till he had finished it, that he might open his note. We are very much delighted when we receive letters from Gawar, especially your Journal, which I always read.

" Yesterday, we were invited to Mr. Stoddard's to tea. In the evening, we all played, 'Button, button, who's got the button?' Once, when Mr. Stoddard was *judge*, thinking that it was *my* forfeit, he said, 'she must say half the multiplication table;' so *mamma* had to say it.

" A young man in the seminary, named *Iwaz*, died on the last day of March. His disease was typhus* fever, and none of the ladies saw him during his sickness.

" It is, as you see by the date, the 3d of April, and the mountain has been covered with flowers; still, we have had a heavy snow-storm, and sleet, all day. I wonder what the weather is in Gawar!

" My time for writing is up, and I must close,

* So fatally infectious, that it was not deemed expedient for any to visit his room, except those who were needed to take care of him.

with love to Mr. Rhea, Mr. Coan, Sanem, and Alexander and yourself.

"From your affectionate friend,

"JUDITH G. PERKINS."

The foregoing note suggests a point that may not readily occur to the youthful reader, namely, that missionaries, in a benighted land, amid the manifold temptations and exposures that surround their children, must be their companions in their little amusements, more than might be necessary in America, where children can be more safely trusted out of the sight of their parents.

"*Oroomiah, April 19th*, 1852.

"DEAR MRS. COAN, — Your welcome letters reached us on Friday night, and as Saturday is rather a busy day with me, I deferred writing until now; and as I hear the messenger leaves to-morrow morning, my note must be short.

"I heard, by one of the letters, that *Shabas* has concluded to remain with you. I was very happy to hear it; for if he had left you, and you had had all the work to do, besides *teaching*, I am afraid you would have been sick.

"*Ansep* [the Nestorian nurse] has gone to the feast, and has not yet returned. In her absence, I have made all the bread, and washed and wiped all the dishes.

"This morning, we all took a very pleasant ride to *Sheikh hill.* Perhaps some of you have seen it, and I will not describe it. Mamma sends love, but is too tired to write.

"I must close, with love to you and all.

"From your affectionate friend,

"JUDITH G. PERKINS."

The faithful old Nestorian nurse, *Ansep*, referred to above, had long resided in the family, and become most devotedly attached to the children, especially to Judith. Being now in poor health, she remained with her friends several weeks, when she visited them at the Nestorian festival of Easter. Since Judith's death, she states, with many tears, among other recollections of her, that the kind and thoughtful child charged her, on leaving, not to hasten back, nor come until she should be recruited and quite well; as she herself was able, and desired to do much of the work in the family, during her absence.

Judith's father and little brother visited the missionaries in Gawar, as early in the spring as the mighty barrier of snow would allow them to cross the high range of mountains, already mentioned. They reached the new station, some of the way through two and three feet of snow, on the first day of May. Their visit is referred to in the note which follows. Mr. Coan returned with them to Oroomiah, on business.

"*Oroomiah, May 15th*, 1852.

"DEAR MRS. COAN,—I intended to acknowledge your kind note by *Kallash*, but as I was somewhat expecting Mr. Coan, papa, and Henry, at that time, I thought I would wait and send a note by Mr. C.

"Sabbath before last being the first Sabbath of the month, we had our missionary meeting. I think we raised one *tomon*, six *sahib korans*, and five *shâhis* [about three dollars and a half]. Some one said, that we raised more than they did at Geog Tapa, this time.

"I presume that Henry has told you all about our *botany* class, so I will not recapitulate,—but perhaps he has not told you about our Sabbath school. The school is opened by singing,—then Mrs. Stoddard prays, we next say our hymns, and then our Bible lessons. We are now studying the life of Christ. For every perfect lesson, we are marked four.

"Yesterday I saw an anecdote in one of the papers, which is quite amusing. Henry wished me to write it down for you to tell to Alexander. A lady, Miss Mix, was trying to teach a little child. She had got him *clean* through the alphabet, and ba, be, bi, etc., and now had put him into syllables of *la-dy*, etc.; and was trying to make him understand the meaning of *syllables.* In order to interest him, she said, 'you love pies, don't you?' 'Yes ma'am.' 'Apple *and* pie, put together, make what?' 'Apple-pie.' 'By a like rule, *la and dy*, make *lady.* You understand?' 'Yes ma'am.' 'Mince *and* pie, spell what, then?' 'Mince-pie.' 'Well! pumpkin *and* pie?' 'Pumpkin-pie.' 'Then what does *la-dy* spell?' '*Custard pie*,' said he, with a *yell* of delight.

"Mr. Coan spent last Sabbath at our house. We enjoyed his visit very much. When Henry came home, he had a great deal to tell us. He described your *house* to us. I hope the ground will soon be dry enough for you to live in tents; though I am not sure you will be much more comfortably situated.

"I was somewhat disappointed, in your not coming down with Mr. Coan, but hope you will come soon.

"Henry told me that you rode once on my pony, while he was in Gawar. I hope you enjoyed your ride.

"My note is rather longer than I intended it to be,—so I must close, with love to Mr. Rhea, Sanem, and Alexander, and hoping that you will accept much for yourself.

"From your young friend,

"JUDITH G. PERKINS.'

The *house* of the missionaries in Gawar, mentioned in the foregoing note, was a rude mud hovel, which would not be deemed fit for a stable in America. They were subjected to extreme annoyance from smoke and vermin, and great exposure from dampness, during their winter residence in that hovel.

"*Oroomiah, June* 18*th*, 1852.

"DEAR MRS. COAN,—Please accept many thanks for your kind note; and though it is acknowledged so late in the day, I hope you will excuse it, as it is very warm, these days. I can hardly do any thing, most of the time, but sew and knit and practise on the seraphine. I must not forget to tell you, that a little while since, the music books, which Mrs. Wright sent for, reached us safely.

"Last Monday, a Russian gentleman arrived at the city. He came up to Seir, on Tuesday morning, to breakfast, and stayed with us until the next morning. His name is Khanikoff. He has been on the top of Mount Ararat. His tent remained two days between the two Ararats. He makes great Ararat to be about seventeen thousand feet high. When on the top, he and his party kindled a fire, and it sunk in the snow.

"We have cherries now. They are very fine. I wish you could have some. Why will you not come down and make us a visit?

"We hope, next Monday, (if we can obtain horses,) to go to Gavalan; so I must stop and finish some mending, on my dress and stockings, or I fear I shall not get them done. The stockings which you gave me, last year, were a little too large, but they do very well, this summer.

"I cannot give you Henry's description of *your house* now, but will try to do so next time.

"Please give much love to Mr. Coan, Mr. Rhea, and Alexander.

"Your affectionate friend,
"JUDITH G. PERKINS."

The visit to Gavalan, above referred to, was made principally for the benefit of Judith's health and that of her mamma. Mr. Stocking's family were spending a few months at that village, which is about forty miles distant from the city of Oroomiah, as a health retreat.

With these notes to Mrs. Coan, we insert the following one to Miss Rice, which possesses a melancholy interest, as being the last that Judith ever wrote,—at least, the last that has been recovered. Miss Rice was spending the summer in Mr. Stocking's family, at Gavalan.

"*Oroomiah, Aug.* 11*th*, 1852.

"MY DEAR MISS RICE,—Please accept my thanks for the very pretty seraphine-stool, which you were so kind as to give me, on my twelfth birthday. Mr. and Mrs. Stocking reached here late on Monday evening. They are with us at tea, to-night, and hope to return to-morrow, so I must hasten.

"We all enjoy our school very much. Yesterday, a box came from America, containing some things for our school, and a telegraph model for Mr. Stoddard.

"Please give my love to Miss Fisk, and accept thanks and much love for yourself.

"From your affectionate friend,

"JUDITH G. PERKINS."

CHAPTER VI.

HER SOCIAL TRAITS.

Few are more *social*, in their disposition and character, than was Judith. She was ever exceedingly delighted to receive visits from the children of the mission, even the youngest, and to visit them at their homes. The "little dinner," or humble collation on a cricket, surrounded by the young group on the carpet of the earth floor, was the height of her entertainment; on such occasions, a blessing usually being implored, at the commencement of the juvenile meal. She was very active, prompt, and skilful, in furnishing agreeable plays for the lively children, which is a problem, not always of easy solution, in the quiet retirement of a missionary's home.

Though an equal companion with the smallest child, Judith was not less interested, in listening to the conversation of the gentlemen and ladies of the mission, in their social intercourse. Indeed, she was singularly qualified, for one of her years, to enjoy their society and participate in their conversation.

The occasional visits which the mission received from travellers, and other European gentlemen, were very deeply interesting events to her. Such visits, in the remoteness of the mission station at Oroomiah, are few and far between; and in proportion to their infrequency, are they welcome to the missionary exile, whether parent or child. Judith always retained the most vivid impressions of every such individual who visited the station, and seemed studious to improve the opportunities, thus presented, to obtain new information and add to her attainments; and no visitor to Oroomiah would soon forget that missionary child.

The visit of the distinguished Russian scholar and traveller, Chevalier Khanikoff, mentioned in one of her notes to Mrs. Coan, is such an instance. He is one of the Russian Emperor's counsellors of State, at present stationed at Tiflis; a gentleman whose exalted official rank, and vast and varied acquisitions as a profound Oriental and scientific scholar, can hardly be surpassed by the amenity of his manners, the modesty of his demeanor — emphatically, the modesty of genius, — and the kindness of his heart.

During his visit of a day at Mount Seir, the parlor of Judith's home was extensively arrayed with his barometers, thermometers, etc.; and so engrossed was he, in making and recording observations — watching his instruments with the alertness of a vigilant sentinel at his post, that he was necessarily obliged somewhat to curtail his social intercourse, though by no means unsocial in character. Some member of the mission playfully remarked, on this subject, that *ladies* must not expect to command a large share of the time and attention of such a *savant*. In allusion to that remark, Judith said to her mother, " Why, I *think* he is a *very* interesting man." Her characteristic discrimination saw so much to admire, in the ardent devotee to the cause of science, that she was exceedingly eager to catch every word that fell from his lips; and to her mamma, who was more or less occupied with domestic cares, she would say, " Come, let us hasten and finish our work, and not lose what he says."

She was especially interested in his graphic account of his ascent of Mount Ararat, which he made in August, 1850. With inexpressible delight, she listened to his statement of the almost inconceivably magnificent views he enjoyed, when standing on the summit of the sacred mountain, according to his careful measurement 16,935 feet above the level of the ocean; how his eye roved away, from that lofty, hallowed observatory, to an immense distance in all directions — to the great Caucasian range on the north; to the Erzroom mountains, two hundred miles distant, on the west — over the central Koordish mountains on the south, and the regions about the Caspian on the east. And lively indeed was her sympathy with the feeling he expressed, that the deepest impression made on his mind, by any thing on the venerable mountain, was, that of *the awful, unbroken* SILENCE *that perpetually reigns there!*

In this connection, it is proper that we record Chevalier Khanikoff's kind sympathy with Judith's bereaved parents. In writing to Mr. Stoddard, after the death of his youthful admirer, he says, "I beg you to have the goodness to present my kind regards to Mr. and Mrs. Perkins, and say to them how much I have shared in the sad and unexpected loss that has befallen them."

The last visit of this kind, which the missionaries at Oroomiah received, before Judith's death, was that of the English and Russian commissioners, in settling the boundary between Turkey and Persia, who, in the progress of their surveys, spent a few days at Mount Seir, a short time previous to that melancholy event. With the estimable Colonel Williams and Colonel Tcherikoff at the head of those commissions, and some ten or twelve very intelligent, accomplished, and amiable gentlemen associated with them, the whole party was a very select one, and would have been such in any land. They were in two instances the guests of the missionaries, where they rendered themselves exceedingly agreeable and entertaining; while they, in turn, seemed equally to prize the privilege of social intercourse with the families of the mission, especially after living three years in tents, far removed from the civilized world, on the rugged and desert boundary.

Mr. Loftus, the geologist of the party, came fresh from several very interesting Scripture localities — from the ruins of "Shushan the palace;" and the tomb of the prophet Daniel; and from the supposed "Ur of the Chaldees," the early home of the patriarch Abraham, at which places he had made many important discoveries. He had with him a great number of very striking impressions and copies of inscriptions and sculptures, from those remains, which he kindly exhibited to the families of the mission, to their unspeakable gratification.

Judith had more than once read Layard's "Nineveh and its Remains," and often inspected specimens collected by her father on the venerable site of the prophet Jonah's home, and studied the subject with an interest and intelligence, that had prepared her fully to appreciate such an entertainment. Her enjoyment of the visit of these gentlemen was quite indescribable. The only abatement to it seemed to be, her apprehension, that her size and appearance, so much above her years, might not be sufficiently guarded by the mantle of modesty — an apprehension, however, which was felt by no one so much as by herself.

Mr. Stevens, the British consul at Tabreez, and his brother, are also among the estimable and agreeable visitors at Oroomiah, whom Judith remembered with much interest.

Of the missionaries of other fields, whose visits and acquaintance she had enjoyed, were the venerable Dr. Glen, translator of the Bible into Persian; Messrs. Stern, and Sternchus, of the mission to the Jews at Bagdad; Mr. Marsh, of Mosul; Rev. John Bowen, a delegate of the English Church Missionary Society; and Mr. Sandreczki, of the same society, who is stationed at Jerusalem. To the last-named friend, who passed several weeks at Judith's home, in feeble health, she became strongly attached, and after his visit, corresponded with his little daughter, who was about her own age. We here insert a note from Anna Sandreczki, and after it, Judith's reply.

"*Bonja, (near Smyrna,) Aug. 13th,* 1851.

"Miss Judith G. Perkins:

"My dear friend, — Your loving letter gave me great pleasure. It is a long time since dear father came from his journey. He has told us many things of you, and how much kindness you have shown him. I would be very happy to become acquainted with you and your little friends.

"Our dear father has often had the fever, since he came from the journey; but I hope the Lord will soon deliver him from this evil.

"The nice books that you sent us, gave us great pleasure. My sister and I will be glad if the trifles we send you, are acceptable, as marks of our sincere love. For you, the larger sewing-box; and for your brother, one of the pocket-books, with the paint box; for dear little sister Stocking, the other sewing-box; for her brother, the second pocket-book. We should like to send you something nicer, but you will not measure our love by this. We shall soon go to Jerusalem. Yesterday the news came from London.

"Give my respects, and my sister's, to your dear parents, and all the ladies and gentlemen of the mission; love to your dear brother and all the other children, whom we love, like you, without knowing them.

"I remain your affectionate friend and sister,

"ANNA SANDRECZKI."

From Judith to Anna.

"*Oroomiah, Feb. 27th*, 1852.

"MY DEAR FRIEND, — Your precious note gave me great pleasure; and I hope you will accept my sincerest thanks for the sweet, pretty present which you and your sister so kindly sent me. I intend it to stand on the centre-table, in the parlor, and when I look at it, I shall think of you, dear Anna, whom though I have not seen I yet love.

"In your note, you speak of going to Jerusalem. I suppose you are now there. It seems as though one could hardly realize, that it is the same city where David, 'the sweet singer of Israel,' reigned; and where king Solomon built that beautiful temple; and above all, where the Saviour spilt his precious blood for sinners. Will you please write and tell me how that ancient city looks now?

"Since your dear father was here, many changes have taken place in our mission. Mr. and Mrs. Stoddard, with their little daughter, Harriet, and Mr. Rhea, have reached us in safety. A mission station has been established in Gawar, a mountain district. Mr. and Mrs. Coan, and Mr. Rhea are residing there. There have been additions also to the children of our mission, since your father was here. Mrs. Cochran has a little girl, named Caroline, and Mrs. Stocking has a little son, named Ezra, and Mrs. Wright has a little son, [not then named].

"My note is becoming rather long, and I must close, with love to your dear parents, and your dear sister and brothers, begging you to accept a large share for yourself, from

"Your affectionate friend,

"JUDITH G. PERKINS."

Judith's strongly social disposition was strikingly manifest, in the seclusion of her missionary home, in the feelings which she cherished towards her relatives in America. She loved her grand parents, uncles, aunts, and cousins, with an ardor, and often conversed respecting them, with a vividness and fervor, that could hardly have been surpassed, had she grown up among them. She deeply sorrowed, whenever she heard of the sickness of any of those relatives, and heartily mourned for those of them who died. On her parents' receiving intelligence of the dangerous illness of her grandpapa, she burst into tears, and sobbing said, "Oh, I fear I shall never see my dear grandpapa again." She generally cherished the hope, as has been stated, that she should, some day, go to America, to see her kindred; and the thought of failing to see that peculiarly loved one, deeply distressed her affectionate heart. That grand parent died, a year and a half before her death, and doubtless welcomed that youthful object of his fond love on earth to the Saviour's presence in heaven.

The little tokens which were, from time to time, sent to Judith, by her relatives in America, were received with very affecting expressions of gratitude, and preserved with nicest care. But her interest in the absent and the distant, was by no means *limited* to her relatives, though cherished so strongly towards them. Many other kind friends in America had shown an interest in her, and sent her good books, and other precious tokens. The names of such friends, though personally unknown to her, became household words with Judith, and though often repeated by her, it was almost as often with the tear of love and gratitude starting in her eye. As an illustration of this point, we may mention a single case, quoting again from the letter of Miss Fisk to Mrs. Reed. "I need not tell you what flower, in our happy circle, has withered on earth, to bloom, as we trust, in heaven; nor what family circle is clothed in deepest mourning. I seem to hear you say, *has my own dear Judith been removed from earth?* Yes, my friend, that dear child whom you loved, and who so tenderly loved you, as an unknown, yet well known, friend, has gone from us. Around us are the tokens of your interest in her; but her sweet voice echoes not back the lively gratitude which she ever felt toward you. That little box of play-blocks, your first gift, and still unbroken in number, with each remembrance, down to the sweet dress in which we lately saw her robed, are still with the bereaved mother, and will not soon cease to call forth the grateful tear from bleeding hearts."

The gratitude cherished by her towards Mrs. Reed, as mentioned in this extract, is only an instance of what she felt and expressed toward all her unknown friends and benefactors in America.

Judith's love for the members and families of the mission, and especially for the children, seemed to know no limits. To the parents, she looked up with a tender, affectionate, and confiding regard, surpassed only by that toward her own father and mother; and their little ones, all younger than herself, after Mr. Holladay's family left the field, she loved and cherished, as though all were her brothers and sisters. And it is hardly necessary to state, that her own tender, confiding feelings ever met a warm response, in the bosoms of all those missionary parents and children. Said Mr. Stoddard to her father, when the latter was about starting with his family, to meet the reinforcement from America, having in charge little Sarah Stoddard, "I feel an unspeakable relief, by this arrangement, in regard to my child, and especially, as she will be with *Judith*, on the road."

A beautiful infant daughter of Mr. Cochran, born just a week to an hour after the mournful event of Judith's death, bears the name of *Judith Perkins.*

As referring to some of the traits of her character, presented in this and the preceding chapters, we here insert a letter, containing reminiscences of Judith, addressed to her father by Mr. Rhea, of Gawar, some time after her death.

"With melancholy delight, I call up reminiscences of a brief but very happy acquaintance with your beloved Judith. I well remember when I first met her, surrounded by a group of her young companions, moving among them like a tender guardian spirit, inventing for them youthful sports, settling their petty difficulties, and diffusing a spirit of peace and joy, throughout the happy circle.

"On further acquaintance, I saw that this spirit of tender superintendence and guardianship, over her little missionary brothers and sisters, was a distinctive trait in her lovely character.

"During the few months spent at Seir, being frequently a guest under your hospitable roof, it was my privilege to become quite intimate with Judith. Her uniformly gentle, happy, and social spirit, her uncommon musical talent, the skill and taste of her youthful performances, her rapid progress and ardent enthusiasm, could not fail to enlist at once the lively interest of a stranger. How sweet were those hours, when, led by Judith, with her much loved seraphine, we sung the songs of Zion! They were ever welcome and joyful, and their zest was not a little enhanced, to see with what fervor of spirit and whole souled earnestness, she animated every strain. Judith will not sing with us here again. She will not come to us, but we shall go to her. The 'new song' she has learned before us, and she may yet, in joyous strains, again lead our voices, when we stand with her around the throne of God, and for the first time join in the melody of heaven.

"I love to think with what delight and characteristic energy Judith welcomed the suggestion of a *missionary association*, among the children of the mission. Her young heart could not contain its ardor; but she felt that she must impart it to her young companions; and the first Monday of the next month witnessed the assembly of the happy children, their eyes intently gazing upon the map, picturing the dark homes of the poor heathen, and their little hands grasping the coin, earned by their own self-denial, to scatter over those dark regions the beams of light and life and joy. Judith loved, from her heart, those little missionary gatherings. She loved to give that whose cost she felt; and we fondly hope, that those youthful expressions of tender sympathy for the perishing nations were pledges of a life, had she lived, one day to be wholly consecrated to their eternal welfare.

"An absence of ten months again brought me to Judith's home. A marked change had passed over her. Her form had grown tall and slender, her mind had made rapid advances in knowledge, and, under the moulding influences of the Divine Spirit, we hope she was rapidly preparing for the rest of heaven.

"I was delighted and surprised, as she modestly referred to her reading and studies during the past year, showing me several large volumes which she had read, and relating from them, in language unusually chaste and select, for one of her tender years, incidents which showed that she read, not to beguile the passing hour, but to enrich her mind with stores of abiding wealth. One who then saw her ruddy cheek, and light, elastic step, would have little thought that the silver cord would so soon be loosed. Ah, how soon and how gently was it loosed, and her fettered spirit freed, to bask in the joyous light of heaven! Thus soon did the night come, and cast its dark mantle over the sweet joys and felicities of our earthly intercourse! Thus soon did the morning of an eternal, blissful day dawn on Judith's glad spirit, and leave us in tears to travel the few remaining stages of this weary pilgrimage, until for us too, if faithful, 'the day will break, and the shadows flee away.'"

CHAPTER VII.

RELIGIOUS INFLUENCES, AND INTEREST.

THAT Judith was, all her life, under strong religious influence, need hardly be stated, when it is recollected that she grew up in a Christian mission. In addition to the care of her parents, and especially of her mother, on whom, in the ever pressing missionary avocations of the father, her moral as well as intellectual training primarily devolved, she had enjoyed the prayers, the solicitude, and in some cases, the personal religious conversations and exhortations of her parents' associates; though doubtless to a less extent, than if it had been apprehended by any, that she was so soon to be removed beyond the reach of their exertions.

As illustrations of the kind interest of those missionary associates, in Judith's salvation, we here insert two notes addressed to her by Miss Fisk and Miss Rice, on two of her birthdays. The first one, from Miss Fisk, was addressed to her on her eighth birthday.

"*Oroomiah, Aug. 8th,* 1848.

"MY DEAR JUDITH,—It is not convenient for me to accept your kind invitation to spend your birthday with you; but I shall often think of you, and hope that you may have a very pleasant time with your friends. While at home, I will ask God to bless you, and make you one of his *own little children*, before another birthday comes. I am sure that you do not think you are too young to begin to love the Saviour. Is not eight years long enough to live in sin? Then will you not give all the rest of your years, be they few or many, to *Him* who loves little children better than their fathers and mothers can love them?

"With this, you will find two little *hair-bands*, which I wish you to accept as a token of the pleasure I have felt, in seeing you try to please your mamma, in using such bands.

"My kindest love to your papa and mamma, and Henry, and many a kiss to your sweet little sister.

"Yours in love,
"FIDELIA FISK."

The following note from Miss Rice was addressed to Judith on her eleventh birthday. It possesses peculiar interest, as having been found, after her death, in the basket she used to hang on her saddle when she rode, with the appearance of having been often perused.

"*Gawar, Aug. 8th*, 1851.

"My dear Judith, — I have just been writing Mrs. Breath, and the date reminds me, that this is your birthday. I will indulge my inclination to write you a few words. I hope this will be a happy day to you, and that this year, which you have now commenced, may be the happiest one of your life. Do you know the sure way to be happy? I long to have you know how sweet it is to be at peace with God, and how blessed it is to have the Lord Jesus for the guide of your youth, and the guide of your life, and your guide to glory at last. How many times has He sent the Spirit to you, inviting you to seek a home in heaven! Will you not heed those gentle whisperings? Will you not look at your heart, and see how much you need just such a Saviour as Christ, to make it clean? Will you not pray, 'Create within me a clean heart?' Is hall hope to hear from you, when the messenger returns.

"Your true friend,

"M. S. Rice."

The following is Judith's note, in reply to Miss Rice.

"*Oroomiah, Aug.* 15*th*, 1851.

"DEAR FRIEND AND TEACHER,—I am very much obliged to you, for the little note which you was so kind as to write me on my birthday. I think I must tell you something of the entertainment we had on that day. In the afternoon, there was no school. At dinner, we had company. All were here, except Dr. Wright, who was at the city. We took tea at Mr. Stoddard's, and spent the evening there.

"We have a very pleasant school, [taught a few weeks by Mrs. Coan]. Maps hang all around the room. We all have desks except Alexander, and there is a dunce-block which stands under the teacher's table.

"Mrs. Cochran has been very sick, but is now better. Sickness and death are always at hand. I desire that in this, my new year, I may be a good girl, and be prepared for death.

"Accept this from your affectionate pupil,

"JUDITH G. PERKINS."

Letters from Mr. Rhea, of Gawar, to the children of the mission at Oroomiah, had also deeply interested Judith. The following is one of those letters.

"*Memikan, Gawar, Feb.* 14*th*, 1852.

"TO JUDITH AND ALL THE CHILDREN:

"My dear Young Friends,—It is now getting

late, (Saturday evening). I have written a good deal, to-day, to my older friends at Oroomiah, and I thought I could not let the messenger leave, on Monday morning, without a line to my little friends, of whom I love to think, and for whom I love to pray.

"I would like to have you all come up to Gawar, very much. I think you would be pleased to look over this beautiful plain, and upon these great mountains, all covered with snow. The wolves howl very much, some nights. They come quite near, sometimes; but you would not be frightened while staying in the house. I think you would like to see the little girls come into Mrs. Coan's room, so clean and nice; I mean their faces; for they are poor little girls, and have not fine clothes; and their mothers will not wash their coarse ones.

"I think, too, you would like to go into the *Dickana*, (the elevated part of the stable,) and see the little boys, reading in their testaments. Each one has a little sack for his book, and before he comes to school, washes his hands very clean; and some of them have as many as two or three thumb papers, so that their fingers do not touch the leaf of the book at all.

"Sometimes little Joseph and Jenga and Khamis come and sit down on the floor, by my stove. I love to have them come and talk with me. They have all learned the Lord's prayer very well; and Joseph says, that he and his brother Khamis repeat it, every morning when they rise, and every evening when they lie down. Joseph says, too, 'we do n't revile now, since we come to school and learn to read. Our mother reviles, but we tell her not to revile; that it is wrong.' They are the sons of a widow — their father having died several years ago. They are very poor, but are very pretty little boys, and are learning very fast. Would you not like to teach such little boys and girls? I hope that, some day, this may be your pleasant work. Would it not be delightful to you, to meet one little boy or girl in heaven, who should say to you, 'you taught me to read the word of God; you told me about Jesus?'

"May God bless each one of you, my dear little friends. May you all be like lambs, in the flock of Jesus — gentle, and kind, and harmless; and may you all be very happy in your homes, in your studies, and in your little plays and sports with each other. A kiss to each of you — and a sweet sleep to-night, and a happy Sabbath day on the morrow.

"Ever your friend,

"S. A. Rhea."

To Jerusha Stocking, one of Judith's little companions, the same kind friend of the children wrote, about the same time, as follows: "Suppose you had a great and good friend, and that every time you entered his room, he would smile upon you and embrace you in his arms; and if there was a tear in your eye, wipe it away; or if your heart was swelling with grief, soothe and comfort you; or if sick, would watch, day and night, without weariness, at your bed-side, giving you healing medicines. Suppose that his words were always kind and gentle, and that whenever you saw him, he would ask you if there was any thing you would like to have, and would look upon you with such winning love, as would make you ask him for what you wished.

"Oh, if there was such a wonderful friend, would you not love to look upon his face, to rest upon his bosom, to hear his gentle words, to sit with him, to walk and talk with him; and would you not go very often to his room, and put your hand in his, and ask him to be your dear father, and friend, and guide? Oh, I know you would.

"But there *is* such a great and kind friend. Yes, you already know who he is; Jesus, the good Shepherd, so gentle, that He is called a Lamb; so strong, that He is called a Lion; and so loving, that He is called the 'altogether lovely.'

"'But where shall you find him?' perhaps you will ask. Why, there is no place that you can go where he is not. Only fall upon your knees, and He will be by your side.

"It was a long time before I found this dear Friend; and at last I learned, that wherever I went, He went with me; and that I could not take a step if He was not by my side; and that His kind hand had given me every good thing that I had. Then I was sorry that I had never taken notice of Him, when He had always been so near. I hope that you will not grieve Him by such treatment, and that you will go to Him and tell Him that you wish to love Him as long as you live."

In some of her notes which we have inserted, Judith mentions her Sabbath school. She was very deeply interested in this Sabbath school, which was under the care of Mrs. Stoddard. The exercises consisted of a psalm, committed and recited in the language of Scripture, by each pupil, and a hymn by each one, after which a parable, or some other passage of the New Testament, was read by the children in turn and explained by the teacher, each child being questioned on the meaning. "The Child's Hymn Book," published by the American Tract Society, was the one from which the pupils usually selected their hymns. Judith's copy, presented to her by Miss Rice, and doubly prized by her for the giver's sake, has a great many of the hymns pencilled at the top, by Mrs. Stoddard, with the child's initial, and a number indicating that it was perfectly recited. This book is among the many and affecting memorials of the departed one, that now meet the eyes of the bereaved parents, to solace their stricken hearts, as well as remind them of their loss. Her fondness for hymns led her often to commit two for the Sabbath school, instead of one as required for her regular lesson.

Of her attendance at Sabbath school, Mrs. Stoddard thus speaks: "Judith was ever perfectly consistent in her deportment. Once or twice, she was induced to smile, by the levity of one of her companions; but soon the blushing face and silent tear told her sorrow. Her lessons were always well prepared, and the interest she ever manifested made it a pleasure to teach her. Her influence in the school was very happy on the other pupils, as a model, inciting them to correct conduct and perfect recitations."

She was accustomed to recite her lessons, once or more, to her mother, before going to Sabbath school, and she often repeated many of the hymns afterward, in the family, and with an intensity of interest and emotion, that beamed most impressively from her beautiful eye, and irradiated her whole countenance with an almost unearthly fervor. One hymn, which is remembered by her parents as often thus repeated, is the following:

"Little travellers, Zion-ward,
Each one entering into rest,
In the kingdom of your Lord,
In the mansions of the blest;
There to welcome, Jesus waits,
Gives the crowns his followers win;
Lift your heads, ye golden gates!
Let the little travellers in!

"Who are they, whose little feet,
Pacing life's dark journey through,
Now have reach'd that heavenly seat,
They had ever kept in view?
'I, from Greenland's frozen strand;'
'I, from India's sultry plain;'
'I, from Afric's barren sand;'
'I, from islands of the main.'

"'All our earthly journey past,
Every tear and pain gone by,
Here together met at last,
At the portal of the sky,
Each the welcome, "come," awaits,
Conquerors over death and sin.'
Lift your heads, ye golden gates!
Let the little travellers in."

The juvenile missionary concert at Oroomiah has also been mentioned. This too was a matter in which Judith was very deeply interested. It was commenced by Mr. Rhea, and continued by Mr. Breath after Mr. Rhea removed to Gawar. The money, contributed by the children, is devoted to the support of a Nestorian missionary to Bootân, a mountain district about three hundred miles west of Oroomiah, on the ancient river Tigris, where the poor, scattered Nestorians are as sheep without a shepherd. Judith felt a very lively concern in the welfare of those Nestorians. She was not only willing, but happy to deny herself of as many table comforts as her parents would allow her to dispense with, as also to perform any domestic tasks assigned, to save money for the missionary concert, and thus aid in sending them the gospel.

Deacon Gewergis, the "mountain evangelist" of Tergaver, who preaches in the nearer mountain districts, frequently visited Judith's home, to report his tours to her father, who had the particular direction of his labors. The good man's visits were always hailed with joy by Judith. Being supported by the avails of the Nestorian monthly concert at Seir, to which she also contributed, he was familiarly called by her, "our missionary." His placid smile and benignant countenance, and his "glad tidings," could be greeted with no more hearty welcome by any member of the mission, than they were by that missionary child. To cheer the way-worn, indefatigable evangelist's heart, and remind him of his promised rest in heaven, she was ever delighted to entertain him, a few minutes, during each visit, with a sweet piece or two of music on the seraphine.

It hardly need be said, that this mountain missionary was very deeply afflicted by her death. Silence, and suppressed sobs, were the only expression he could give to his feelings, for a long time, on visiting her saddened home, in the first instance, after that event, to tender his sympathy to the bereaved parents.

Judith's interest in the cause of missions, was of early growth. When quite a small child, she often spoke of becoming a *missionary*, and was then particularly interested in *China*, as a prospective field of labor. And to the last, she always seemed to assume, that she should be a missionary somewhere, if her life were spared. Reading the memoirs of female missionaries, as the memoir of Harriet Newell, and that of Mrs. Dwight and Mrs. Grant, and of Mrs. Van Lennep, and others, served to quicken that desire, and strengthen that impression; and her circumstances on missionary ground, naturally kept the subject fresh before her mind. She said to some of the older Nestorian girls of the seminary, the last time she ever saw them, and only four days before her death, "I hope, after I return from Erzroom, to study very hard, and afterward go to America, and attend school awhile there, and then return and be a missionary here; or, I would prefer to go and labor where there are no missionaries."

In an important sense, Judith *had long been a missionary helper.* She ever manifested a very deep interest in all the departments of the good work among the Nestorians, and sought to aid in its progress in every way in her power. She had sat patiently many an hour, and assisted her father in adjusting the verses of the translation of the Bible according to the English version; reading the latter verse by verse; and she seldom seemed happier than when aiding him in that great work, which she longed to see accomplished. During the last year of her life, she assisted her mother in teaching a few Nestorian females connected with the Sabbath school, and eagerly engaged in the loved employment.

The female seminary was the department of the labors of the mission, in which she seemed to feel the deepest interest. She often visited it, and sometimes pursued her studies, a few days, in connection with it, lodging with her kind friends, Miss Fisk and Miss Rice, and being taught by them. She was always familiar with the names of the thirty or forty pupils, and in most cases, with their character and standing; and she ever heartily rejoiced in their progress and improvement. None could feel greater delight than she did, in marking the striking and happy change in them, from the ignorant, listless, and ragged girls, — their mouths "full of cursing and bitterness" — as taken from their homes, to the intelligent and refined young ladies, and many of them devotedly pious, under the divine blessing on a few years of arduous missionary toil expended upon them. She had sometimes expressed a desire to become qualified to teach in that favored seminary.

Judith was in turn ardently loved and admired by those Nestorian girls. Many of them emulated her example and repeated her words with most affectionate deference. Their grief, on hearing the tidings of her death, was almost inconsolable. In the language of Miss Fisk, "no event has ever so deeply affected them as Judith's death."

Let not the friends of the sacred cause in America suppose that funds, expended on *such* missionary daughters, are lost to that cause. No mortal, except those who were thus favored, can conceive the comfort, solace, and support, which she afforded, for many years, to her toil-worn parents, aside from her active exertions to relieve and aid them in their domestic cares and missionary labors.

Among the religious influences, which strongly affected Judith's feelings and character, should be mentioned the removal by death of three of her brothers and her two sisters. In bereavements, as in all the economy of Divine Providence, rich and precious mercies are mingled with severe trials. In the painful experience of not a few parents, it has doubtless been found, that the sore "chastening" of parting with their offspring, for the present "not joyous but grievous," has not only worked in *them* "the peaceable fruits of righteousness," but has also been the means of spiritual blessing to their surviving children.

Judith was accustomed to think and speak of her departed brothers and sisters as *living* in heaven. She remembered and noticed their returning birthdays, kept their respective ages, and cherished a lively hope and expectation of dwelling forever with them, when she should die. Such an anticipation, long and fondly, and even earnestly cherished, could not fail deeply to strengthen her interest in eternal things.

Among the reminiscences of those dear departed ones, which interested her, was a sweet piece of poetry, written by a kind missionary brother, on the death of the second infant child whom her parents laid in the grave, in the form of a dialogue, between that brother and an infant sister gone before him. Judith often read that piece of poetry; and as an interesting memento of her, in regard to her love for those deceased brothers and sisters, and her desire to be with them in heaven, we here introduce it entire.

"To the Rev. J. and Mrs. C. B. Perkins, the following lines are affectionately inscribed by their sympathizing missionary brother,

J. L. Merrick.

Tabreez, July 28th, 1839.

THE INFANT'S CALL.

Brother cherub, come away!
'Tis thy sister spirit calls;—
Join our blissful, bright array,
Where the sweetest glory falls.
Around the Saviour's blessed throne,
Who for us infants did atone.

Beauteous angel, let me stay,
In affection's tender arms;
What should tempt me now to stray?
Strangers fill me with alarms.
O, dost thou know a parent's love,
And all the filial joys I prove?

Brother, brother, dost thou know,
Who it is that calleth thee?
Thy own sister, spared all woe,
By going home in infancy!
Thy parents are *my* parents too,
And loves were ours, as now with you.

Lovely spirit, can it be,
Thou so beautiful and bright,
Art akin the least to me,
Filled with pleasure and affright?

Perfection seeming half divine,
Beams awful thro' those smiles of thine.

Darling brother, do not fear,
Gentler than a mother's care,
Free from every sigh and tear,
Is the kindness you shall share.
And all that in *me* now you see,
Soon, soon, dear brother, thou shalt be.

Angel, what will brother say,
When he finds that I am gone!
Who will cheer him day by day;
Meet him smiling as the morn?
Ah, why should he be left *alone,*
And I removed to worlds unknown!

Lovely brother, do not call
Me an *angel,* with awed tone;
I'm *thy sister,* loving all
Thy fond heart proclaims its own.
You need not love our dear ones less,
For sharing heavenly happiness.

Lovely sister, is it true?
In our circle then remain;
We will share our joys with you;
You shall lead our blooming train.
How happy then we all shall be,
Sweet seraph sister, here with thee.

Well I know the silken ties,
Twining round your little band;
And the tide of sympathies,
Flowing full on every hand.
But, know, the golden chains above,
Are infinite, eternal love!

Dost thou know how near our birth?
  Five* baptized, one blessed hour!
Let us bloom awhile on earth,
  Twining in affection's bower.
O why should such a beauteous wreath,
So soon be marred by ruthless death?

Dearest brother, I was there,
  With an infant angel band,
Hymning, in the hallowed air,
  Him who baptism did command.
Come! we 'll oft return and see,
The dear ones now detaining thee.

Dearest sister, much inclined,
  Still I cling to those below,
Where my heart has fondly twined;
  Other worlds I little know.
You must be very happy there;
Erelong may we your glory share.

Brother, lift thine eyes above!
  Seest thou Him in smiles divine?
Image of eternal love;
  O how sweet his glories shine!
Behold, he comes, what raptures swell,
At thy approach, Immanuel!

Sister, bear me on thy wing;
  Let us meet him in the skies!
Look! I 'm like thee! How they sing;
  Louder, sweeter, as they rise!
Hail! O my Saviour and my Lord!
By infant hosts untold adored."

* Five infant children, in the Nestorian mission, whose births occurred within a few weeks of each other, were baptized together.

Judith's little sister, Fidelia, the last of the two infants whom she herself followed to the grave, died three and a half years before her own death. She most ardently loved that sister, and had taken inexpressible pleasure in tending and caressing her; and the separation made a much more vivid impression on her mind, than the death of those of whom she had only heard, and of the one who died when she was quite small; but it also gave a reality and an interest to them all, in her mind, which she had never felt before. From that time, she was more than ever in the habit of thinking and speaking of her five brothers and sisters in heaven, as a *united group*, which she and her parents and little brother still on earth, were at no distant period to join. And many a time, in the quiet of the evening hour, and under the mild glories of a Persian sky, she has gone with her parents, or with her brother Henry, to Fidelia's grave, in a Nestorian cemetery, on a beautiful hill, a few rods from her home, and there thought and spoken tenderly of that loved band, in the world of bliss, and longed to be with them.

For several years she had been exceedingly anxious to go to Tabreez, a city one hundred and forty miles distant from Oroomiah, which was the first residence of her parents in Persia, mainly, so far as she was concerned, to visit the grave of her sister Charlotte, their first-born. That long and fondly anticipated privilege she never enjoyed; but she had often visited the little graves of her three brothers in the city of Oroomiah, and shed the tear of affection over them.

But of all subjects and objects, interesting to Judith, the *Saviour* was the one that most tenderly affected her young heart. She was ordinarily very buoyant, lively, and playful, to the close of her life; but this theme, when mentioned, would ever touch and engross her feelings, and call them off from all other things. She was never encouraged by her parents, or others, publicly to profess religion, or confidently to indulge the hope of being a Christian; but her whole appearance, during the last few months of her life, was such as strongly to warrant that hope for her; and had she lived, she would probably soon have become a visible member of Christ's flock. An earlier and more definite direction of her thoughts to such a profession, might doubtless have contributed more rapidly to develop and mature her religious feelings and character. Her mother, who ever cultivated an intimate acquaintance with her feelings, has generally thought, that she gave quite satisfactory evidence of piety, from early childhood.

Many interesting incidents come to the remembrance of Judith's parents, since her death, which occurred during the last few months of her life, and which are now recalled as indicating the strong current of her thoughts toward heaven. On the last night of her last year, for instance, she proposed to her mother to close the retiring year and commence the new, in prayer, after the manner of a Methodist watch-meeting. This was devoutly done, one petition offered being, that "the coming year might be the *best year* of her life."

We will not linger to multiply such incidents, but may remark in general, that her peculiarly subdued, lovely spirit and demeanor, during those last months, observed by others as well as by her parents, and the deep interest which she manifested in the religious exercises of reading the Scriptures and prayer, with her mother, especially so during that period; and most of all, her wonderfully interesting appearance on her death-bed, yet to be described, all point to an inward, progressive work of preparation for her last conflict, of which none were perhaps fully aware, till it was strikingly and delightfully developed in the trying ordeal.

In looking over her books and papers, a short time after her death, her parents found on her slate, on which she was accustomed to write notes for copying, the following lines: "O that I were a Christian! How happy I should be!

How happy my dear mother would be! And would it not be pleasing to God? *Why am I not one?"* This pencilling had no date, but was probably written not long before the commencement of the journey on which she died; and these were perhaps the last sentences she ever wrote. He who will not break the bruised reed, nor quench the smoking flax, had, we doubt not, regarded her earnest desire here expressed, (though by no means now *felt* for the first time,) to be a lamb of His flock, and adopted her among the chosen of his fold. Her change, as in all cases of conversion, was of course instantaneous; but its precise date she may not have been able to specify; and its outward development, as is often the case, especially in one of so lovely a temperament and character by nature, was gradual, like the rising light.

CHAPTER VIII.

JUDITH'S LAST JOURNEY.

In the foregoing pages, we have often spoken of the subject of this memoir, as *little Judith.* Liability to a mistaken impression, in regard to her size, from the use of that term, should perhaps again be mentioned, though forestalled in the preface. She was large of her age. Though but a little more than twelve years old, she had reached the height of about five feet, being nearly as tall as several of the ladies of the mission. She was of a delicate form, and regular and very comely features, united with singular ease, grace, and gentle dignity of manners; her whole person and appearance being that of remarkable symmetry and maturity, which were the true index of her mind and heart and entire character.

Of her appearance when she started on her last journey, Mrs. Stoddard writes as follows: "Her womanly bearing on the day she left us, was remarked by many. In her kind attentions to her mother, her care for her brother, and

At the age of twelve years.

her farewells to her little companions, one would not have recognized the girl of only twelve years. Methinks I see her now, as she went with light footsteps to this room and that, looked into this bag, or opened that trunk, to be sure that every thing was placed as her mother had directed; then I hear her sweet voice, speaking of her bright anticipations of her journey, the pleasure she would receive from meeting new friends; and see the sparkle of her eye, as one scene after another came before her imagination. Then, after the tearful 'good by,' how nimbly she glided into the carriage, to ride to the city, preparatory to mounting her pony, over which she had more command than many of twice her years."

A member of the mission remarked, after her death, that "had Judith known, when she left her home and started on her last journey, that she should never return, her whole appearance could not have been more interesting, or more grateful to the recollection of those from whom she then parted."

The last affecting scenes of Judith's short life, which we now approach, we shall give mainly from the touching letter of Miss Fisk to Mrs. Reed, already quoted, and from a concise memorandum from the pen of her father, sometimes, for convenience, combining passages from the two, which refer to the same subject. Miss Fisk says: "It would have been a great comfort to all our circle, if this loved one had died with us, and we have been permitted to ease one sorrow, when the pangs of death took hold upon her. It would have been a sweet privilege to us, to have caught the last accents that quivered on those lips, and standing beside the swelling stream, seen her, as it were, pass over, and join the happy ones, calling 'Sister spirit, come away.' But this might not be. As if it were not enough for the little pilgrim, that she had twice crossed the wide waters, been borne once and again over the rugged mountains of Armenia, and stood on the dizzy heights of Koordistan, she must leave us, and die in a strange place. The tender parents and loved brother were by that dying bed; but no missionary brother or sister might whisper to the afflicted ones, 'Jesus is a present help.' Ah, why must it have been so? When we think of it, we can only feel, that the Saviour would show to this dear brother and sister, that His love and His grace were sufficient, in walking through the fiery furnace.

"You will ask, what called these friends from the circle who love them here? The approach of Mr. and Mrs. Crane, and little Sarah Stoddard made it necessary that some one should go to Erzroom, and help them on their way. Providence seemed to point to Mr. Perkins as the one to go. He at first shrank from it; nor did we wonder, when we recollected how many toilsome, not to say perilous, journeys, he had performed. Mrs. Perkins's health had for some time been very poor, and we had all felt, that a change in her case was strongly called for. We hoped that a journey to Erzroom might benefit her, and it was recommended to Mr. Perkins, by our whole mission, that he should take his family with him. Judith and Henry were particularly happy, in the anticipation of the journey. They thought of meeting little Sarah Stoddard, from whom they had been separated by so painful a providence; and Judith exceedingly longed to look on old Ararat's snow capped summit, and to feel that she was near the spot where righteous Noah once dwelt. Dear child; she saw the goodly mountain from afar; and then, as we believe, went up to the sacred hills of light, to be forever with the Holy patriarch.

"A few days before the time fixed for leaving, Mrs. Perkins became very unwell; and the parents were full of doubts, in regard to leaving their home. Judith nursed her mamma most tenderly, and begged her not to relinquish the idea of going, saying that she could and would relieve her of all care. Her feelings greatly helped her parents to feel happy in undertaking the journey."

The commencement of the journey, we give in the language of the memorandum of Judith's father.

"On Monday, the 30th of August, 1852, I started with my beloved family, to meet Mr. and Mrs. Crane and little Sarah Stoddard, at Erzroom. I had felt a great reluctance to undertake the journey, having often been over the long and weary road, and being very desirous that the printing of the Old Testament should not again be interrupted. The prevalence of cholera at Oroomiah during the summer, from which we had been graciously preserved at our health retreat, had also created in my mind a mysterious misgiving at the idea of separating myself, or seeing any other one separated, at such a time, from the society of our missionary circle, not knowing what a day might bring forth. That feeling, which I sometimes chided in myself as a weakness, I was nevertheless quite unable to banish. But when the mission finally appointed me to go, as no other member seemed to find it practicable to do so, and with the understanding that I should take my family for the benefit of Mrs. Perkins's health, I was reconciled to the arrangement, and even enjoyed the prospect of the journey, experiencing a peculiar relief, in surrendering my own judgment and preference to the general decision.

"Mrs. Perkins and our children rode to the city with Mr. Stoddard, in the carriage. Accompanied a short distance out of the city, by Messrs. Wright, Breath, and Cochran, on horseback, we proceeded, and reached the *bridge*, three hours distant, just at dark, all of us having greatly enjoyed the horseback ride over the charming plain. There we passed a comfortable night, and starting with the dawn,

"*Aug.* 31*st*, we reached Gavalan between nine and ten o'clock, A. M. Mr. Stocking met us a few miles out of the village, with his waggon, and took in Mrs. Perkins and the children. We passed a most delightful and refreshing day at Gavalan, in the bosom of our kind friends there, and completed some arrangements for the journey."

Of the travellers' stop at Gavalan, Miss Fisk says, "I was at the time with Mr. Stocking's family, and it was to us a most delightful privilege to have them spend most of Tuesday and the following night with us. We spoke of the pleasure the visit had given us, on the succeeding days; but we little thought, nay, we thought not at all, that it was our *last visit* with Judith, till we should commune with her in 'heavenly places.' We were all deeply interested in the dear girl. She was lively and happy; and yet she seemed to us to have a kind of chastened joy, and a peculiar sweetness. For every little kindness she was very grateful; and I remember, just before she left us, she asked me in a whisper, 'Do you think that I have ever thanked Mrs. Stocking as I ought, for her kindness to me, when I was here last summer?' When I told her I thought she had, she said, 'I am very glad if I have; but if you are not sure, I want to do it before I go away.' In every thing, she seemed peculiarly thoughtful and tender of others; and her short stay with us confirmed us in the impression, that the last few months had wrought a great change in her.

"Our dear friends left Gavalan, Wednesday morning, September 1st, a happy family, and with the prospect of a pleasant journey. We heard nothing from them till Sabbath evening. Then a letter was handed to us, which, when opened, almost overwhelmed us. It was a pencilled one, written from *Zorava*, a Mohammedan village about one third of the way from Oroomiah to Erzroom, on the afternoon of September 3d, and contained these sad words: 'I write you in deep waters. Our precious Judith is just gone of *cholera*. She was taken about one o'clock to day, within three or four miles of this place. I can say no more. The precious, dying one is in my arms. Pray send to the city, and come and meet us. Farewell. J. PERKINS.' I will not stop to tell you of our feelings, but return to our dear pilgrim friends, now indeed in 'deep waters.'"

We here turn from Miss Fisk's letter to the father's memorandum, as being more full.

"*Sept.* 1*st.* We left our dear friends at Gavalan, near nine o'clock, A. M. Mr. Stocking again carried Mrs. Perkins, Judith, and Henry, a few miles, in his waggon, to help them on their way, that they might thus be gradually initiated to long stages on their saddles. Our ride over the high mountain, between the province of Oroomiah and Salmas, was delightful. Judith was greatly interested in the charms of the wild and rural scenery, and the beauties of every object of nature. The stage of about thirty miles was performed with great ease and comfort to the whole party. At Yavshanly, where we stopped on the plain of Salmas, not far from the north-west corner of the lake, we had a nice place for our tent, on a green meadow near shade trees, and were in every respect most comfortable, during the afternoon and night.

"We started the next morning, September 2d, a little after dawn. We halted to rest, a few moments, on the top of the mountain which separates the plain of Salmas from that of Khoy. Judith ran up a hill-side, to obtain a last view of the lake, precisely where the late Mrs. Stoddard lingered, about four years before, for the same purpose, the last time she ever saw it, and only about a month before she died of cholera at Trebizond. Every object on the way seemed to possess the deepest interest to Judith, even the bare, sterile mountains; and her enjoyment seemed inexpressible. The isolated mountain of salt on the one hand, and the tomb of the Mohammedan saints, perched on a lofty eminence, on the other, were among the things that engaged her attention, in turn, and beguiled the sameness of the long and weary ride.

"I often inquired, on the road, whether there was *cholera* at Khoy, and was as often strongly assured there was *none*; and being informed, that the arrangement, requiring passports, at the boundary, would henceforth be rigorously enforced, I took the route by the town, to obtain such papers. We reached Khoy about midday, after a ride of more than thirty miles, and passed around to the Erzroom gate, where we sat down a half hour under an umbrella, just without the walls, till our tent was pitched. We passed the afternoon very agreeably, the only annoyance we experienced, arising from the crowds that flocked around us to gratify their curiosity. At evening, persons came to us requesting medicine for *cholera*, which startled us, as it assured us that the disease was there."

We here return to Miss Fisk's letter. "They saw that they were breathing pestilential air, and were where, perhaps, many were falling. There was no alternative, however, but to spend the night. They committed themselves to Israel's Keeper, and lay down to rest. A broad, hot plain was before them; and anxious to avoid the heat, they arose very early the next morning. They had worship, at which Judith repeated from memory the 54th Psalm, the same which she had recited at Sabbath school, on the previous Sabbath; and after taking a cup of coffee, they commenced their ride at three o'clock. The bright moon was several hours above the horizon; and the slight haze of the cholera atmosphere, mingling with its mild rays, shed a peculiar softness over the charming scenes always presented on the beautiful plain of Khoy, giving to them an almost unearthly hue. All seemed well, and Judith enjoyed that morning's ride exceedingly, as she had all her journey. She looked with peculiar delight on the morning star, and on the rising sun, now rising on her for the last time; or rather, before another morning, to be swallowed up in the brighter rays of the 'sun of righteousness,' and she to go where she may forever gaze on 'the bright and morning star' of the seed of David. As I tell you of the events of the day and night that followed, you will thank our God anew, that he hides the future from his children.

"After crossing the plain of Khoy, a lofty mountain lay before them, which is crossed by a gradual ascent of ten miles. When about half way up the mountain, they halted for breakfast, it being about an hour after sunrise. On the top of this mountain, they had a view of the summit of Mount Ararat, a hundred miles distant. Judith was filled with ecstasy at the longed for sight, and would have left it reluctantly, but for the hope of enjoying a nearer view in due time. She seemed to her parents to be very well, and in unusually good spirits. She dismounted with the others, to walk down the steep descent, for some distance. Now in sight of the sacred mountain, her joy was so great, that she *must run and leap*, and was the first down. As the others came up with her, she smilingly said, 'Mamma, did you see me run?' She and Henry had sung together on the road, and if perchance a flower nestled in autumnal shades, it shared her loving look, as did each object of nature on that last morning.

"After descending the other side of the mountain, which is much less than the ascent on this side, the little company stopped again for some refreshment. On every face sat a happy smile, and all wished that the friends left behind could know how well and happy they were. Dear friends! They little knew what sad messages they would be called upon to send us, in a few hours more! They had proceeded but a few miles from this last resting place, when Judith spoke of not being well; and her pale face showed more plainly than her words expressed, that she was a sufferer. Vomiting and purging followed, which led her parents to feel very anxious in regard to her; and they would have stopped at once, but their tent had gone forward. They could not rest under the burning sun, and there was no water near. They were therefore obliged to proceed three or four miles farther, to the village of *Zorava*. Their anguish, as they trod that weary way, may be imagined, but not described. Judith grew sicker and sicker, and the symptoms of that fearful disease, the *cholera*, more and more marked. It was with difficulty that she reached the tent; and as she was lifted from her horse, in a state of great exhaustion, will you wonder, that the parents almost sunk, under the sad prospect before them, in the lonely, inhospitable village of *Zorava?* Can you realize the sorrow of your and our friends, on that day, far away from their loved home, and with scarce a comfort for a sick and dying one? These were bitter hours to them, and rendered doubly so, by the unkind Mohammedan villagers, who would not allow a morsel of bread to be sold to the faithful Nestorians who accompanied the family, nor even barley, for their tired, hungry horses. And more; when the limbs of our dear Judith were cold, and even stiffening under the power of the deadly disease, they would not sell one stick of wood to warm water for her; but once and again ordered the heart-stricken travellers to leave the village with their dying child. May the rejected Saviour forgive those followers of the false prophet; for they knew not what they did!

"The bitter cup was closely pressed to the lips of our friends, on that afternoon; but its ingredients were not all wormwood and gall. He, who tasted sorrow for us, was there, and the sick one was calm as a summer's evening. She had not a fear in regard to the result; not one complaining exclamation to make. During the whole afternoon, she was perfectly conscious, her mind clear, and working with more than its wonted vivacity and energy; while her countenance, beaming with rays divine, lighted that lonely tent."

CHAPTER IX.

PROGRESS OF THE DISEASE, AND DEATH.

We now return to the father's memorandum, for a more particular account of the progress of Judith's disease, and her feelings in the near prospect of death. He says: "On arriving at the tent, my anxiety was intense, which Judith must have perceived, but she was not at all agitated by it, and only remarked quietly, 'I wish Dr. Wright was here.' As soon as possible, I opened our medicines, and gave her laudanum; but she very soon vomited. We gave her camphor, which was also thrown off; and there were frequent purgings. No doubt could remain, as to the nature of the disease. The word, *cholera*, had not been mentioned in her hearing; but Judith now meekly inquired, 'Papa, do you think it is cholera?' She was, however, still perfectly calm and composed, though aware of my apprehensions, having evidently been prepared for this trying hour, by the grace of God.

"The disease moved on, like a giant, with irresistible force. The frequent and abundant doses of camphor and soda, which we administered, produced not the slightest perceptible effect, and the vomiting, in some instances, much distressed her.

"Soon after reaching the tent, I requested Judith to fix her eye and her heart right on the cross of Christ, and keep them there; to which she replied, calmly and firmly, 'I will try, papa.' I frequently repeated the same direction, and received the same reply. With her eyes often closed, she was obviously thus engaged; while I, in my solicitude and anguish, could not suppress audible, ejaculatory prayer, a good deal of the time.

"After administering laudanum twice, in my haste I set down the very small vial containing it, among other things in our deranged tent, and could never afterwards find it, though I searched the tent over and over, with an anxiety amounting almost to distraction. In the absence of laudanum, I administered all the paregoric which we had on hand, which doubtless did as well as laudanum would have done; but in those circumstances, I could hardly forgive myself for not having kept the laudanum bottle in my hand.

"Mrs. Perkins, who had never before witnessed a case of cholera, and was at first not so sure as I, that such was the disease, tried to quiet my feelings, for some time, till she too saw unmistakable signs of the awful reality. We continued to administer camphor, and soda water, the latter being very grateful as a drink to the dear sufferer, who was parching of thirst.

"By this time, our two Nestorian attendants, and the Mohammedan muleteer, were gazing into our tent, with surprise and deep concern. The disease still rapidly advancing, like a strong man armed, I despaired of its being arrested, and directed Hormezd, (one of the Nestorian attendants,) to try to find a messenger for Oroomiah. He found a man who promised to go, and with Judith in my arms, I scratched the line which I afterwards forwarded. Mrs. Perkins said to Judith, 'We are going to send home; would you like to see Dr. Wright?' 'O what joy!' was her expressive reply. But the villagers, in their fright at the cholera, suddenly brought so near them, now interposed, and forbade any one going as our messenger.

"All this time, Judith maintained perfect calmness, and enjoyed peculiar clearness of mind, as she did indeed throughout, evidently leaning on more than a mortal arm. Once when I asked her, 'Dear Judith, is Jesus precious to you?' 'O yes,' she replied; 'I have just had a view of Him; O how lovely!' What a balm was that reply to our writhing hearts! At another time, I inquired, 'Dear Judith, have you a desire to get well?' She replied, 'O, yes, papa, if it be God's will.' 'Why, dear Judith?' I inquired. 'That I may do good,' she answered. 'And if it is His will to take you now to Himself, are you not satisfied?' I inquired. 'O yes, papa; His will be done,' was her reply.

"Once she broke the silence by saying, 'If I die, mamma, you will bury me by the side of Fidelia, will you not?' 'O yes, dear Judith,' was the answer. Our great distance — one hundred and forty miles — from home, naturally raised the inquiry in her mind, whether she could be carried on horseback and buried by the loved one of her departed brothers and sisters, who had last died.

"About this time, Henry, who from sadness had been long outside, came into the tent in great anguish, and exclaimed, 'O Judith, my dear sister, I am afraid you will die; you look as though you would die. O dear sister Judith, what shall I do?' crying convulsively. Judith gazed on him earnestly, and with yearning tenderness, but without agitation. Her mamma inquired, 'Dear Judith, what do you wish to say to Henry?' 'O that he may be a *Christian;* and a good boy, and mind his parents in every thing; and stand up straight;' was her reply. The last-named point had been repeatedly mentioned in her hearing, when in health. Her reference to it, naturally suggests, how the smallest matters of conduct assume an importance, in the light of an opening eternity.

"All this time, the vomiting and purging were going on, though at less frequent intervals; her pulse had now nearly disappeared; and her eyes were fast sinking back in their sockets. As evening came on, and a light was brought into our tent, O how did those dark circles, around her bright eyes, contrasting so vividly with her pallid, sunken features, like dark halos encircling bright stars in the sky, point us to the fearful result as near at hand! Her mind was now very clear, and very quick in its operations. Her eyes were unnaturally bright, now turned intently on us, and anon raised upward. To every inquiry which we made, she returned a prompt reply, deliberately and distinctly uttered, like the clear echo from a sepulchre. Perfectly conscious and composed, there was, at the same time, something very peculiar and striking in her appearance; the vivacity and elasticity of a spirit, ready to break away from its earthly fetters, all plumed for its upward flight. Indeed, it almost seemed as though an angel had found its way into that lonely tent, clad in the hues of a departing mortal.

'Her home was far, O far away;
The clear light in her eyes,
Had nought to do with earthly day;
'Twas kindled from the skies.'

"The subject of a messenger was again introduced, and an arrangement finally made for one to go *immediately*, though, as it afterwards appeared, he lingered in the village until morning.

"I often repeated the direction, as I have said, 'Dear Judith, keep your eyes and your heart right on the cross of Christ; let nothing divert you from it; and beseech Him to prepare you for His glory, whether it be in life or in death.' 'I will try to do so, papa,' was her usual reply.

"Collapse had now fully settled upon her, and the disease was much less active. But erelong she exclaimed, 'Oh, mamma, what ails my limb?' How did that inquiry pierce through our hearts, recognizing it, as we immediately did, as referring to a *spasm!* Exhausted ourselves, we called in the Nestorian attendants to rub her lower limbs, which were now much cramped, and they were soon relieved by the friction. We also managed to kindle a fire, of some dry weeds, (the frightened, cruel villagers refusing to sell us wood,) and heated a stone, which we kept at her feet. The night air was cold in that high region, though the sun, during the day, had been very hot, and every aspect around us was most dreary, except as we looked upward. To add to the gloom, a bear, or a wild boar, (the darkness prevented determining which,) sallied down from the neighbouring mountains, and prowled around our tent. Our muleteer proposed to fire on him, but I had notice of his design in time to prevent it.

"Almost crushed with anxiety, I stepped out for a moment, while the Nestorians were rubbing her lower limbs, and Hormezd embraced the opportunity of my absence, as we afterwards learned, to inquire, 'Judith, where do you feel distressed?' She replied, 'Oh, don't ask me that; it is God's will; let His will be done.' The attendants were both exceedingly impressed with her sweet submission and resignation, and with tearful eyes, they said, on their return to Oroomiah, 'we never saw any thing like it.'

"Being now free from pain, excepting when a spasm seized her limbs, she conceived that there might be a favorable change, and once inquired, 'Papa, do you not think there is a reaction?' 'I fear not, my dear,' I replied; 'look right to Jesus, and nowhere else; He is the physician for soul and body.' 'I will try, papa; I *do;* I can trust in Him;' was her reply.

"Her affection for her parents seemed to strengthen, as life waned. 'Sit close to me,' she would say to us, 'and keep your arms over me.'

"Once the silence was broken by her saying, 'Papa, you will take care of *my little tree*, won't you?' 'Yes, dear Judith; where is it?' I replied. 'In the front yard,' she answered. In the rush of her thoughts to her dear but now far off home, they thus lighted, for a moment, on her favorite little tree, as one of the loved objects there; but this, and her request to be buried by the side of her sister Fidelia, were all the earthly requests that she made, if indeed the latter can be thus designated. Her soul seemed too much swallowed up in the Saviour, and the bright prospects before her, to think much of earthly things.

"About this time, her papa and mamma kneeled over her and prayed in succession. She remained silent a few moments after we closed; and then, without any suggestion from us, uttered the following short prayer, slowly and distinctly, and evidently from the depths of her soul—'O Lord, accept me; if it be thy will, make me well again; if not, oh let me not murmur.' We responded an audible *amen*.

"The active form of the disease now having ceased, she lay, some of the time, in a kind of slumber, though she was probably not asleep. Once, as her mamma was feeling her cold hand in vain for any sign of pulse, and despairing, said, 'Oh *must* we then part with her?' she promptly and distinctly replied, 'Oh no; I am not going now. She said this obviously to comfort her distressed mother. In this semi-slumber, there was occasionally a symptom of wandering. I now inquired of her, 'Do you not think you will die, dear Judith?' 'Oh no; not now,' she replied; 'I have just seen an angel, who told me that he had been sent for me; but that I am allowed to stay a little longer; oh, I feel so comfortable I know I shall get well.'

"The anxious hours rolled on, while we still sought in vain for any indication of returning pulse, or symptom of the 'reaction' for which she had inquired; and her feet, hands, and face were becoming deadly cold. For the most part, however, she continued rational, and promptly replied to our questions, in a clear voice and collected manner. Once, observing me feel long and carefully for her pulse, she inquired, 'Is there no hope?' I replied, 'the saying is, "there is always hope while there is life," but I see very little.' She still manifested no fear nor agitation. An occasional spasm in her lower limbs was now her only suffering, and that was soon relieved by the prompt rubbing of the kind Nestorians.

"At length, when we had remained silent a few moments, she said, 'Papa, do repeat something.' I repeated the 23d Psalm, 'The Lord is my shepherd,' etc.; and then inquired, 'Did you understand me, dear Judith? Is it precious?'

'O yes,' she replied; 'O how precious.' I then repeated the verse of the hymn,

'Jesus can make a dying bed,
  Feel soft as downy pillows are;
While on his breast I lean my head,
  And breathe my life out sweetly there.'

I also repeated verses of other hymns, all which seemed to afford her great satisfaction and comfort.

"By and by, restlessness ensued, with occasional wandering. She mentioned Mr. and Mrs. Cochran, as though near her, and asked, 'Why has Mr. Cochran left so soon?' She also asked, 'Has Dr. Wright come?' She remarked, about this time, when I was speaking to her, 'I cannot now hear with this left ear;' and soon afterward, 'Why, is this ear going to be deaf?' She often asked, 'Papa and mamma, are you near me?' (the light being dim, and perhaps her sight also failing); 'Keep close to me; O what a comfort it is to have you by me.'

"At length she said, 'Papa, I think I have *pleurisy;* I feel a *pain in my side.* Dr. Wright once gave me a *Seidlitz*, when I had pleurisy; won't you, mamma?' Her mamma prepared and gave her a *soda powder*, which the dear child called *Seidlitz*, and repeated, on drinking it, 'O how refreshing. Twice afterward, she requested

Seidlitz, and took a tumbler of *soda* in her own hands and drank it, with hearty expressions of satisfaction and gratitude; vividly reminding us of her high enjoyment of every comfort on this journey, and her gratitude for it; and indeed on the whole journey of life. Far enough from being tired of life, she had ardently loved and exquisitely enjoyed its every blessing, as a heavenly Father's gift.

"We knew that the *pain in her side*, which she had mentioned, was the token of rapidly approaching death — *the loosening of the silver cord.* Her breathing now became labored; her voice husky; and her articulation very difficult. After some time, she said, 'Papa, please raise me up.' This was her last audible expression. I raised her up, and her mamma now waked Henry and called him to her. The poor child had spent his tears, and now stood, trembling and silent, before his dying sister. I said to Henry, 'Kiss your dear sister, ask her to forgive you, and say, farewell.' Henry did so; and with a sweet smile, she nodded her forgiveness and farewell. I then requested Henry to promise his sister, that he would try to be a good boy, and do in all things as she had requested him. He did so; and she again nodded her hearty satisfaction, an angelic serenity beaming from her lighted countenance. This was her last recognition. Breathing shorter and shorter, for fifteen or twenty minutes, she gently slept, as we believe, in Jesus, at three o'clock, A. M., on the 4th of September, 1852, aged twelve years and twenty-six days.

"There was not a gasp, nor struggle, nor groan, nor the distortion of a feature, in the dying scene; a termination of the loved one's course, very comforting to the riven hearts of her parents, as had been the remarkable clearness and activity of her mind, and equally so, her calmness, composure, resignation, and firm trust in her Saviour, and the absence of all signs of fear, during her very brief but violent sickness. Eternity never appeared to us so near as at the moment of her exit; its curtain seemed lifted up before us. Nor had death ever appeared to us so disrobed of its terrors. Its Jordan was but a rill, that might be crossed by a single step. Never before had we witnessed so striking a comment on the beautiful hymn:

'Sweet is the scene, when Christians die;
When holy souls retire to rest;
How mildly beams the closing eye;
How gently heaves th' expiring breast!

'So fades a summer cloud away;
So sinks the gale when storms are o'er;
So gently shuts the eye of day;
So dies a wave along the shore.

'Triumphant smiles the victor's brow,
  Fanned by some guardian angel's wing;
O Grave! where is thy vict'ry now,
  And where, O death, where is thy sting?'

"Thus suddenly passed our sweet Judith away! We sat and wept over her a few minutes, the Nestorian attendants most tenderly weeping with us; and I then led the sorrowing group, still retaining the same position, to the mercy-seat, in the *Syriac language*, that the Nestorians might unite with us in the prayer. I afterward directed them to retire and sleep, while we closed our loved one's eyes, and then lay down by her side, not to sleep, but to weep, to pray, and to praise."

CHAPTER X.

RETURN AND FUNERAL.

We continue the memorandum. "In the morning we rose, much exhausted by the affecting scenes through which we had passed, and had a cup of coffee prepared to strengthen our prostrated bodies. As we were drinking it, by the side of Judith's lifeless remains, Henry burst into tears and said, 'Oh, I wish this were the time when Christ was on earth, to raise the dead!" and after a few sobs, he added, "O that we had not left our dear home; then perhaps Judith would not have died!'

'She slept upon the shroud, on her white bed,
Amid the weepers. There was none to say,
Talitha Cumi; or uplift the head,
That in its flood of silken tresses lay
Scarcely dishevelled; with so slight pain
The dark-robed angel waved his fearful rod,
And from the beauteous clay that knew no stain,
Drew forth the pure in heart to see her God.'

"As I walked a few moments around our tent, soliloquising in bitterness of spirit, — 'What has come upon us?' etc., I observed that the tent was pitched precisely on the spot where I had pitched our tent for a night seventeen years before, with the lamented Dr. and Mrs. Grant, and Mr. Merrick, our first missionary fellow-laborers, when I was conducting them to Persia from Erzroom, whither I had been to meet them. The thought of two of those friends, long since arrived in glory, as having perhaps welcomed thither the spirit of our darling Judith, who bore the name of one of them, and whom we had just given back to the Saviour, on the spot where, long ago, I kneeled in prayer with those missionary pilgrims, threw a double sacredness around the place where I stood, and sweetened my cup of anguish.

"Though well nigh crushed, we had sorrowful duties still to perform. After seeking help from above, the mother, with her own hand, clipped a few of those 'silken tresses,' to keep herself, and send to far off friends. And then with her own hands she washed the corpse, and dressed her own child for the grave. As no coffin could be obtained, the loved one was sewed in a strong oriental felt, of the size and form of a bed-quilt, and placed upon her bed. In the absence of other means and other aid, Hormezd, with his dirk, cut two willow sticks from the margin of the brook, and sewed them upon the sides of the bed, to which the dear form was lashed, and then bound to the back of the faithful horse.

"A long parley, most trying in such circumstances, must now be held by me, with our Mohammedan muleteer, to induce him to return with us. A part of his horses and mules had gone on to Erzroom in another caravan; and a far more serious obstacle urged by him, was, his apprehension lest he, and perhaps all of us, should be mobbed, or even murdered, by outraged Mohammedans on the road, should he be seen carrying the corpse of an *infidel* (Christian,) to say nothing of the violence he would thus do to his own feelings as a *good mussulmân.* An arrangement with the muleteer, who was exorbitant in proportion as our necessity and dependence seemed pressing, being finally concluded, we commenced our mournful return about ten o'clock A. M., the cruel, panic-struck villagers of Zorava still calling on us to 'depart quickly,' and we feeling thankful that we were permitted to leave the place without being *stoned.*

"An hour after starting, we met Colonel Tcherikoff, the Russian commissioner in settling the boundary between Turkey and Persia, and his secretary, who had visited us a few weeks before, at Oroomiah. They were astounded and deeply affected by the sorrowful tidings, and by the sight of us followed by the lifeless remains of our dear daughter, whom they had so recently seen in the bloom of health. They urgently requested to be permitted to do any thing in their power to aid and relieve us. We could only desire them to convey the intelligence to our friend, Colonel Williams, now two days beyond, who was looking out for our approach to his camp, on our way to Erzroom."

We now turn from the memorandum, to the letter of Miss Fisk, for an account of the return of this mourning family to their home. She says: "Retracing the steps of the previous day, required in them no ordinary resignation and Christian fortitude. As they remembered how the dear departed one had then cheered them on their way, and now looked on all that was mortal of her, borne in solemn silence after them, they exclaimed in anguish of spirit, '*What hath a day brought forth!*' That sad and weary ride was as naturally as gratefully relieved, by reminiscences of dear Judith; the religious ones being of course the most interesting. Among such, Henry artlessly said, 'Last Sabbath evening, the evening before we left home, as we were walking on the roof, dear Judith said to me, "Henry, perhaps I shall die on this journey; and how delightful it will be, to go up to that heaven, and see God who never dies."' On the day previous to that Sabbath, she had also remarked to little

Harriet Stoddard, with affectionate solemnity, 'Perhaps I shall die on this journey.' On opening her basket, which was hung on her saddle when she rode, and observing among the books which she had put up for the way, 'the Memoir of Wilberforce Richmond,' Henry said, 'About five Sabbath evenings ago, Judith read to me on the roof, about the death of Wilberforce Richmond.' Her mamma could also call up many peculiarly sweet seasons of religious conversation and prayer, which she had recently held with the departed one, all of which were most comforting to their desolate hearts, as strengthening them in the confidence, that she now rested in the Saviour's bosom.

"The little band of mourners reached the beautiful gardens of *Pera* — a large village on the plain of Khoy, about sunset. They had passed those gardens at dawn, on the preceding day, and Judith's young heart had been filled with delight in observing them. Here they remained till midnight, and then came on their sorrowful way, feeling compelled to travel on the Sabbath, on account of the corpse, in that hot region, as also to avoid unnecessary observation, by remaining long at one place.

"As they rode on, they often gave audible expression to their grief. At such times, little Henry, who followed his parents on the white donkey formerly rode by his sister, would call out to them, 'Do n't cry; it is no matter if Judith has gone to heaven; that is a better place;' but the little comforter's own heart would break, the next moment, and weeping most bitterly, he would say, 'Who will walk with me on the roof now? Who will sing with me? Who will play for me on the seraphine? Who will help me get my lessons?'

"With such sad reflections the afflicted ones were borne on their long, hot, and weary way, and reached Yavshanly, a village in Salmas, about midday. On the way, the horse, bearing the corpse, in one instance slipped, in the sidling path, on the very brink of a turbid stream, and fell; and in his struggles, all but plunged down the bank, before the precious charge could be dislodged from his back. It was a moment of deepened agony, to hearts already bleeding at every pore.

"The murky cholera atmosphere struck them as terrible, both on the plain of Khoy and of Salmas, where the disease was raging fearfully; and they were doubtless in imminent peril, while again passing through that atmosphere.

"They were now within a few hours of Gavalan; but as yet we knew nothing of the scenes through which they had passed, their messenger not reaching us till Sabbath evening."

We interrupt the narrative of Miss Fisk a moment at this point, to introduce a note written at Yavshanly, by the bereaved father, to his missionary associates, and forwarded to Mr. Stocking.

"*Yavshanly (Salmas), Sabbath, Sept. 5th,* 1852.

"TO ALL THE BRETHREN AND SISTERS, — We have just reached this village, on our return with the lifeless remains of our dearest, sweetest Judith. She died of *cholera*, at *Zorava*, at three o'clock, yesterday morning. I trust a line forwarded by a messenger from that place, a little before her death, has prepared you for the intelligence of this terrible stroke.

"I cannot now attempt to describe the progress of the destroyer, which resulted in her death in about fifteen hours after the first symptom of disease. Up to the time of the attack, she had been one of the happiest of mortals, all the way on the road, and had travelled with great ease and almost no weariness, often remarking, 'I am not tired at all; how easily I ride!'

"I need not attempt to portray to you the afternoon and night of *agony*, which we passed at the lonely Mohammedan village of *Zorava* — while the king of terrors was tearing from our arms the earthly idol of our hearts. I have said *agony;* but it was the agony of *parental hearts.* The loved one removed was perfectly calm, and perfectly conscious, till nearly the last, often commending her soul to Christ in silent prayer, and once in an audible prayer, uttered from the depths of her soul, which seemed to be illumined and prepared for the awful moment, by light and strength from on high.

" Nor need I say that our hearts are riven and crushed; but we would have them bleed, till Jesus shall heal the wounds He has inflicted. To grace we owe it, to tell you that we have been wonderfully supported and comforted, in a situation more heart-rending than often falls to the lot of mortals.

" I cannot enlarge now. We propose to start with the rising moon, and shall, with God's help, be in Gavalan early in the morning. Be kind enough to send this sheet right along, by a footman or otherwise, to the city. If Mrs. Perkins and Henry could be carried from Gavalan in the waggon, it would be a great relief. I have no occasion, I am sure, to bespeak your prayers in our behalf.

" Most affectionately yours,

" J. Perkins."

Miss Fisk's narrative of their return continues thus from the point where we left it in Salmas. " Mr. Stocking went early the next morning to meet them, and a few hours brought our stricken friends to us. We longed to comfort their wounded spirits; but when we looked at them, in their grief, a voice seemed to say, 'a time to be silent.' The remains of our precious Judith were laid in the deep shades of Mar Yohannan's garden, till evening, when they were borne from us in sweet silence; for even the Mohammedan muleteer, after all his misgivings at first seemed now to feel that he was bearing precious dust to its last resting-place. His remaining apprehensions, if he had them, would of course also lead him to prefer the stillness of night for the completion of the journey."

The arrival of the intelligence of Judith's sickness and death at her home, is thus described in a note to her father, by Dr. Wright, to whom it was first communicated: "We can never forget the morning of the 6th of September, when the announcement of dear Judith's death was first made to us. The day had just begun to dawn. I was in a sound sleep. *Bekky*, the nurse of our little boy, came to the door of our bed-room, and called 'Sahib,' [Sir]; I half waked, and she said in Syriac, 'Judith is dead!' It seemed like a dream. Half bewildered, I rose up in bed and asked, 'What is it?' 'Has anybody come?' 'Is there a letter?' She replied, 'Pera,' (Mr. Stoddard's servant), 'says so.' I told her to call him. She went out, and soon returned with your note, written on Friday, at four o'clock, P. M. I took it to the window, and by the faint light of breaking day, was just able to read, 'We are in deep waters. Our precious Judith is just gone of *cholera.*' It would be vain to attempt to describe the emotions of Mrs. Wright and myself, at this moment. The tears flowed freely. 'Can it be?' 'Can it be?' we asked. I looked again at the note, and marked the words, 'the dying one.' Hope revived. She *may* still live. 'While there is life there is hope.' I at once prepared to hasten to you, and with Mr. Stoddard, Mr. Cochran, and Miss Harris, started for Gavalan. We were hourly looking for another messenger. When about six miles from the city, we saw a footman coming at a rapid speed. On meeting us, he stopped and took from his girdle your letter from Yavshanly. I dismounted, took the letter, opened it with a trembling hand, and read it aloud. Our hopes were all dashed to the ground. The dear one was no more. There by the roadside we stopped and wept. We rode on toward Gavalan with sad hearts. 'The Lord hath done it,' we thought, and were still.

"Monday night, as Bekky (the Nestorian nurse) was undressing our little Caty, the child, crying convulsively, said in Syriac, 'That beautiful, that wise, that loving girl, is dead!'"

Mrs. Stoddard, referring to the same subject, as also to the arrival of the corpse at Seir, as contrasted with Judith's departure from her home one week before, says: "Very different was the scene on that spot, from that of the previous Monday. Now none but sorrowing, anxious countenances were to be met; for tidings had come, that our dear young friend was prostrated with cholera. We did not then know that the fearful disease had finished its work; and in the midst of our anxiety, a hope of better tidings would often arise. But at evening, our first fears were confirmed.

"I cannot describe our feelings, when, on the morning of Tuesday, we saw the lifeless remains approaching our dwelling. The tears and sobbings of our children and of the natives, were heart-rending. We could only look upward and say, 'Our Father doeth all things well.' 'What we know not now, we shall know hereafter.' 'In wisdom hast thou done it.'"

Miss Fisk continues: "The brethren from Seir met our friends at Gavalan, and accompanied them, the next morning, on their way to their lonely dwelling. They reached their home in the afternoon, to be surrounded by a large circle of weeping friends, afflicted in their affliction. The funeral services, which were held soon afterward, were conducted by Dr. Wright at the house in English, and by Mr. Stocking at the grave, in Syriac; and before the setting sun, the dear child was laid on our green hillside at Seir, and by the side of her darling sister, where she had requested to be buried. At the grave, one of the Nestorians who had accompanied the family, by request, artlessly told the assembled villagers the affecting scenes which he had witnessed. All were bathed in tears; for all felt that they had lost a friend. In all the families of the village, she had taken a deep interest; and several of the middle aged women had been taught by her in the Sabbath school. Indeed, she had greatly endeared herself to all the scores and hundreds of Nestorians who knew her, and was a universal favorite among that people. Said a Nestorian of a distant village, on hearing of her death, 'there was none like her; so beautiful, so wise, so pious. She would pray like an angel.'

"The grief expressed by the Nestorians, assembled at her funeral, as they stood by her open grave, was most affecting; and it was a melting sight to all, to see the parents and little Henry, worn out with the fatigue of their long and rapid journey, and with their sorrow, sink down upon Fidelia's grave, and there watch the committing to the dust of their darling Judith."

The services were closed on that hallowed spot, by singing in Syriac, a translation of the following beautiful hymn, which had been a favorite with the departed one, and was one of the last pieces which she played on the seraphine. The Nestorians joined in the singing.

"Sister, thou wast mild and lovely,
Gentle as the summer breeze;
Pleasant as the air of evening,
When it floats among the trees.

"Peaceful be thy silent slumber,
Peaceful in the grave so low;
Thou no more wilt join our number;
Thou no more our songs shalt know.

"Dearest sister, thou hast left us;
Here thy loss we deeply feel;
But 'tis God that hath bereft us;
He can all our sorrows heal.

"Yet again we hope to meet thee,
When the day of life is fled;
Then in heaven, with joy, to greet thee;
Where no farewell tear is shed."

This hymn was printed soon afterward, in the "Rays of Light," the Nestorian monthly periodical, as appropriate to the memory of Judith; and a biographical sketch of her was published in the same number.

CHAPTER XI.

A DESOLATE HOME.

WE continue the narrative by Miss Fisk. "The burial being over, the stricken family returned to their desolate dwelling, to feel anew the breach made in their household. The dear departed one had long been the light and life of that dwelling. The feeble mother leaned on her precious daughter. When sickness invaded her almost worn-out frame, Judith was ever by her side, to nurse — and that most tenderly — the suffering one. Did she ask for society? It was found in this dear child, whose amiability and intelligence made her a pleasing companion to all, and especially, a solace to that mother, on whom so many bereaving strokes had fallen. Did household cares press? This mature child, of twelve years, would kindly say, 'O mamma, let me take all the care; I cannot see you sink; for my life is bound up in yours.'

"Did a devoted father ask a little repose, when borne down with missionary labors? It was always found in *Judith*. That sweet eye, which I am sure you will remember, ever met papa with a smile, and with something interesting in her reading, or with a sweet piece of music. By her side, cares were forgotten, and he returned to his study or other labors, with new interest, and thankful for the roses strown in his path.

"Few brothers depend on a sister, as did Henry on Judith; and I feel for him, as I never felt for any child, in his loneliness. It is a comfort to us to know, that thousands in our native land will sympathize with all these bereaved ones, and tenderly pray for them, when they shall hear what God has done."

We turn once more to the father's memorandum, in regard to the point here presented by Miss Fisk. He says: "My pen refuses to tell the desolation of our home, with dear *Judith gone*. But God has inflicted the dreadful blow, and we would bow silently and submissively under it. No preceding bereavement, and hardly the removal of all those of our children who died in infancy, fell upon us with the weight and severity of dear Judith's death. So fair, so mature, so intelligent, and so amiable, she was, in the eyes of fond parents at least, one of the loveliest of beings; and arrived at such an age, she had become as our right hand, as well as the joy of our hearts.

"It was inexpressibly grateful to us, when the funeral services were over, to yield ourselves up to the kind sympathy of our beloved missionary friends, after all our terrible anxiety, fatigue, and exposure. They kept us at their tables, till the morning of the third day after our return; for we shrank from approaching our own loved board, with that affecting breach staring us in our faces, and but a single olive plant remaining.

"When we finally took our places at our own family altar, for the first time after our return, as we opened our hymn books, Henry pointed us to the 495th hymn, Church Psalmody, and said, 'that is the hymn which Judith selected, and committed and recited at Sabbath school, the last Sabbath she was here;' and it is the one which we sung at family worship, that Sabbath morning. This is the hymn.

'Time is winging us away,
  To our eternal home;
Life is but a winter's day,
  A journey to the tomb.
Youth and vigor soon will flee;
  Blooming beauty lose its charms;
All that's mortal soon shall be
  Inclosed in death's cold arms.

'Time is winging us away,
  To our eternal home;
Life is but a winter's day,
  A journey to the tomb.

But the Christian shall enjoy,
  Health and beauty soon above;
Far beyond the world's alloy,
  Secure in Jesus' love.'

"This incident cheered our desolation; for it furnished fresh evidence, that the current of Judith's thoughts had of late run strongly on such subjects.

"Poor little Henry Martyn was comforted by his dreams. He said to his parents, some time after her death, 'I often dream of Judith.' And to their inquiry, 'What do you dream?' he replied, 'that she comes down from heaven and talks with me.' And to the farther inquiry, 'What does she say to you?' he artlessly answered, 'when I once asked her, "*is* heaven a better place than this?" she said, "O yes, a great deal better;" we were walking together near the gate, and when I looked around, she was gone.'"

Here taking leave of the father's memorandum, we return once more to the interesting letter of Miss Fisk, already so often quoted. Proceeding from the point where we left it, she says, "A great and most unexpected breach has been made, not only in the family, but in our little circle. Judith had passed the dangerous period of childhood, and though delicate, we felt that in her mountain home, she had a fair prospect of growing up; and indeed, having almost reached her mother's height, she seemed to us to stand on the very verge of womanhood. All looked on her with peculiar interest, as the oldest of the missionary children; and the little flock now feel, that their eldest sister has gone, and are ready to exclaim, with little Caty Cochran, only three years old, '*I want to die, and go to heaven and be with Judith.*'

"You know that Judith's education had been conducted almost wholly, by the unwearied efforts of her mother; and that mother had been most richly repaid, for each hour's care, by her eagerness to learn, her rapid improvement, and her tender gratitude. Few at twelve years of age, in any circumstances, possess the general intelligence that was Judith's; and her interest and proficiency, in the study of the Bible, were remarkable. To teach her, was a great pleasure to any one. And as we think of what she was, in this and other respects, we only awake more deeply to our loss.

"Little Henry alluded, on his sorrowful way homeward, to the *seraphine*. This was the gift of a kind friend in America, and it was a great comfort to dear Judith, as well as to others, in their solitude here. She quickly learned to play on it most sweetly, though she had but very little instruction in the use of the instrument. As I write you from Judith's once cheerful home, the now silent seraphine, and a thousand pleasant reminiscences stealing over me, make me feel, that I stand on sacred ground.

"The bereaved parents are wonderfully supported, in their sore trial, though the wounds fond nature feels can never be healed. You will weep with us, when you hear the sad tidings, and we know that you will remember in your prayers, our afflicted circle, and especially the stricken parents, who had before given back to the Saviour five precious little ones; and that brother, who may never again answer to a sister's gentle call. Though crushed beneath this stroke, they can sweetly say with the departed one, 'Let the Lord's will be done.' The experience of that dying bed was such as greatly to console *them;* and more precious, if possible, is the remembrance of her life, and especially of the last few months of it, in which she seemed so rapidly ripening for the rest into which she has entered. It was not fond parents alone that saw and felt this; others who loved the precious one had felt, that she was indeed a lamb of Jesus, and wondered not that such sweet consolations were imparted to her, in a dying hour, under so sudden and fearful a summons. She had loved the Saviour in the bloom of health, and He would not forget her when passing through the dark way that led to Him. We think of her as *blessed — supremely blessed*, and not even the parent would call her back; and yet there are hearts which almost feel what little Caty Cochran expressed, '*I want to die, and go to heaven and be with Judith.*' "

The first time that the notes of the "silent seraphine" were revived, after her death, at Judith's desolate home, by her beloved teacher, the following beautiful hymn was sung, and often afterward, as a solace to the bereaved parents. It is here inserted, as the form in which their feelings, in the hours of their deep but sanctified grief, have found frequent and grateful expression.

"Thou art gone to the grave; but we will not deplore thee;
Though sorrow and darkness encompass the tomb;
The Saviour hath pass'd through its portals before thee,
And the lamp of his love is thy guide through the gloom.

"Thou art gone to the grave: we no longer behold thee,
Nor tread the rough paths of the world by thy side;
But the wide arms of mercy are spread to enfold thee;
And sinners may hope, since the Saviour hath died.

"Thou art gone to the grave; and its mansion forsaking
Perchance thy weak spirit in doubt linger'd long;
But the sunshine of heaven beam'd bright on thy waking,
And the sound thou didst hear was the seraphim's song.

"Thou art gone to the grave; but we will not deplore thee,
Since God was thy Ransom, thy Guardian, and Guide;
He gave thee, He took thee; and He will restore thee,
And death has no sting, since the Saviour hath died."

CHAPTER XII.

NOTES OF CONDOLENCE.

THE remaining pages of this memoir are mainly occupied with familiar notes of condolence, received by Judith's parents, from missionary friends and others, while on their way to their desolate home, and soon after reaching it. They are interesting, as showing the estimation in which Judith was held, as also for the deep and tender sympathy which they breathe, and the rich variety of appropriate words of consolation, addressed to the stricken mourners, which they contain.

Though penned with not the most distant idea of any public use being made of them, we trust that the authors of these notes will excuse their preservation, in the humble casket in which the precious memory of dear Judith is embalmed, whose early and lamented death was the occasion of them.

From Rev. Wm. R. Stocking.

" *Gavalan, Sabbath Evening, Sept. 5th,* 1852.

"My dear Brother,—Our hearts are filled with grief, at the sad intelligence contained in your note of the 3d, which reached us a few moments since. We would fain hope that the precious child may have been spared, though brought so low. May the God of all consolation, and our gracious Saviour, be near to you and sister Perkins, and your other child, in this time of deep affliction. I would hasten to you immediately, if it was thought possible for me to proceed with my eyes, which are bound up, on account of a severe attack of ophthalmy.

"Joseph [a brother of Mar Yohannan,] and another man, start immediately to meet you, and in the course of five hours, your letter will be at Seir, and some one there will doubtless come on without delay. I hope I may be able to start in the morning, but from my severe pain, last night, I fear a night ride, in the present state of my eyes.

"Yours with deepest sympathy and most heart-felt prayers,

"W. R. Stocking."

From Miss F. Fisk.

" *Gavalan, Sabbath Evening,* 5 1-2 *P. M.*

"DEAR AFFLICTED BROTHER AND SISTER,—I write you a line, not only to express my own sympathy for you, but that of us all. Your messenger reached us half an hour ago, and a man has been gone some fifteen minutes, on his way to the city. Mr. Stocking longs to fly to you, and so do I; but Mr. S. has had a hard day with his eyes, and dares not undertake to go in the night. I trust that we shall be able to leave in the morning.

" The intelligence from you came just as we were assembled for our evening Sabbath school, and many here wept with us. We feel almost overcome by the shock, and how much more must you. A Father has done it, which will comfort, but cannot heal your bleeding hearts. We will pray for you, and beseech our Saviour to sustain you; but when I think of the greatness of your affliction, I find that words are few. Precious friends! We have all shared your sympathy in days that are past, and *we feel most tenderly for you in this day of your sorrow.* May it be that the dear child lives? Our hearts cling to the possibility; but with you, the sad reality may have taken away your last hope. Must it be so? The Lord has done right. That must set each thought to rest. O may He comfort you, dear brother and sister, and little Henry too. We shall wait in inexpressible anxiety till the next tidings come. The precious Saviour be with you. He alone can know your feelings, if dear *Judith* has been taken from you.

"Yours in sorrow,

"FIDELIA FISK."

From Rev. J. G. Cochran.

"MY DEAR BROTHER AND SISTER, — I can only say, that my heart bleeds with yours, in the overwhelming intelligence that has this moment reached us. Ours is a circle of weeping and deeply stricken hearts; but what must be your distress and agony of soul! Your darling daughter — your beloved Judith riven from your embrace, and that, on your lonely, comfortless journey! What could be more piercing to your heart, and trying to your faith? Vain is the help of man. The Lord reigns, and shall not the Judge of all the earth do right? It is He that wounds, and it is He alone who can heal. I need not commend you, as your only source of consolation and support, to the riches of His boundless grace and infinite love.

"I am summoned to make preparations for some of us to go and meet you, and trust I shall find it practicable to go myself, and have only time to add the assurance of my heart-felt sympathies, and fervent prayers that a God of love may bind up your bleeding hearts.

"Most truly yours,

"J. G. Cochran."

From Mrs. D. P. Cochran.

"My dear Mr. and Mrs. Perkins, — I feel that I can hardly write. My heart is almost bursting, from the heavy, *heavy* tidings just now come. May God have mercy on you, and succor you, in this hour of deep affliction. Would that some of us could have been near you, and softened by our sympathy the dreadful blow. Nothing has occurred since I have been in Persia, and I may say, in my whole life, that has so taken hold of my sympathies, and made me feel that our only refuge is in God. *Judith*, dear child, was dear to all our hearts. She loved our children, and was as an elder sister to them.

"May your only remaining child be spared, and be brought safely back to us. We long to see you all safe back. Miss Harris goes to meet you, and were it possible, I would go a part of the way. We feel that we are one, and would crave the place of mourners together.

"Yours most affectionately,

"D. P. Cochran."

From Rev. D. T. Stoddard, after the parents' return.

"My dear Brother, — My heart is full. My thoughts, at early morning and late at night, go out to you in the most tender sympathy. If I do not talk with you much about the painful scenes through which you have passed, it is because I know not what to say. No words are adequate to express the emotions of the heart, at such a time. May God be a comforter to you both, and bind up your desolate hearts, and give you his sweet presence, in your otherwise desolate home. May you realize, to the full, the meaning of the promises, and say 'It is the Lord; let Him do what seemeth Him good.' As one tie after another is severed, which binds you to earth, may heaven seem nearer and more attractive. There our best friends have gone. There Jesus is. There too we shall soon arrive. Let us live more for heaven. Let us be dead, and our lives hid with Christ in God; so that when He, who is our life, shall appear, we also may appear with Him in glory.

"Affectionately your sympathizing brother in Christ,

"D. T. Stoddard."

From the mission.

"*Seir, Aug. 8th*, 1852.

"DEAR BROTHER, — The following action was taken by the mission to-day, namely, 'Whereas it has pleased our Heavenly Father, to remove from our circle, the last week, by cholera, Judith G. Perkins, while accompanying her parents to Erzroom, to meet Mr. and Mrs. Crane, under circumstances of very peculiar aggravation,

"'Resolved, That we tender to our beloved and deeply afflicted brother and sister our tenderest sympathy.'

"As secretary of the mission, I was expected to communicate the above action to you; and in doing so, I will only say, that *language* fails to express the sympathy we all feel for you and your dear wife, in your sore bereavement.

"Affectionately your brother,

"A. H. WRIGHT,

"*Secretary of the Mission.*"

The notes which immediately follow, are from English gentlemen, who are very kind friends of the missionaries, and who had visited Oroomiah, and were personally acquainted with Judith as well as her parents.

The first note is from Colonel Williams, who has been repeatedly mentioned in the foregoing pages of this memoir. He was, at the time of her death, near the base of Mount Ararat, about midway between Oroomiah and Erzroom, just closing his arduous labors of many years, in surveying and settling the boundary between Turkey and Persia. He had heard of the contemplated journey of the family to Erzroom, and fondly anticipated seeing them on the way. In a note to Judith's father, dated August 27th, 1852, he playfully said, "I hope we may meet on the road; we willgive you a royal salute." Little did he then think, that within one short week from that time, *dear Judith* would die so near him, — within about two days' ride of his camp — and that he should so soon be called in providence to address a letter of condolence to her heart-stricken parents. Colonel Williams heard of the melancholy event almost immediately, through his colleague, Colonel Tcherikoff, the Russian commissioner, who, as it has been stated, met the bereaved family, soon after they started on their return towards their home.

From Colonel W. F. Williams, R. A.

"*Near Mount Ararat, Sept. 8th*, 1852.

"MY DEAR MR. PERKINS, — I have written fully to-day on your affairs, to Mr. Coan of Gawar. These few lines are to convey to you the sincere expressions of grief and condolence, on the part of myself and the gentlemen of the commission, on the lamented death of your daughter, whose very amiable character has been the theme of our conversation, since we had the pleasure of visiting at Seir mountain.

" Beyond the expression of our grief, it would be ill-timed to offer you any others. We feel sure that your mind, and that of Mrs. Perkins, are infinitely better stored than ours, with those reflections — those sure and certain hopes, which lead to resignation under such a dreadful blow, inflicted by the unerring wisdom of God. We therefore abstain from any such intrusion, but nevertheless, with a fervent hope, that you and Mrs. Perkins, to whom all join in kindest regards, will be supported under your sudden and deplorable loss.

" Believe me yours always faithfully,

" W. F. Williams."

From R. W. Stevens, Esquire, British consul at Tabreez, Persia, a long tried and faithful friend of the mission.

" *Tabreez, Sept.* 17*th*, 1852.

" My dear Sir, — It was with deepest and most heart-felt grief, that we received, a few days ago, from Colonel Williams, the melancholy intelligence of the death of our dear friend, Miss Perkins; and I hasten to offer you the expression of our condolence, and to assure you, that we sincerely sympathize with you and Mrs. Perkins, on the premature removal, from this world, of a person so promising, and possessing so many rare qualities, to make her loss a matter of deep regret to yourselves, and to all who had the good fortune to know her.

"May an all-wise providence, in inflicting on you so severe a blow, spare your remaining son to you; and that he may grow up a pride and a blessing to his parents, is the prayer of,

"My dear Sir, yours very faithfully,

"R. W. STEVENS."

From George Alexander Stevens, Esquire, a brother of the consul.

"*Oct.* 17*th*, 1852.

"MY DEAR SIR,—With the deepest regret, we learn, from Colonel Williams, the severe loss which it has pleased the Almighty to inflict on your family; and I beg to be allowed to offer my heart-felt condolence, on the sad and mournful event. It is one of those decrees of providence, against which we may not murmur, and under which we must bear up with patience and fortitude.

"May the Almighty grant,* to our departed friend, an everlasting abode in his heavenly kingdom; and may we all live in hopes of enjoying such an access to it, as the one who has been so suddenly summoned away from us.

"Pray offer my condolence to your kind lady, and believe me, my dear sir,

"Yours, very sincerely,

"GEO. ALEX. STEVENS."

From C. A. Rassam, Esquire, British consul at Mosul.

"*Mosul, Dec. 4th*, 1852.

"MY DEAR SIR, — Your kind letter of the 17th ultimo is before me, and you have my best thanks for forwarding both the letters and cases to Mr. Brant of Erzroom, and ere this I hope they have reached Constantinople, where Colonel Williams is now residing. The potatoes we also received in safety, nearly three weeks ago.

"I am truly sorry to hear, that the cholera is raging so fearfully in Tabreez, but more especially do we both condole with Mrs. Perkins and yourself, for the severe loss you have sustained, in the death of your affectionate daughter. I

* This estimable friend of the missionaries is a member of the Roman Catholic Church, which will explain the form of his kind expression of sympathy.

can well conceive, that the frequent wounds which you have received are now opened afresh; but Christ can pour into those wounds oil and wine, and be your Comforter. God in his infinite mercy grant, that you may both experience the consolation of the Holy Spirit, and be able to say with pious Job, 'The Lord gave, and the Lord hath taken away; blessed be the name of the Lord.'

"I have just heard from Dr. Lobdell, that your missionary friends in Gawar are in some difficulties with the authorities. If I can be of any service to them, I hope they will not fail to make use of me.

"Deacon Joseph, my brother, has just returned from Bagdad, and expects shortly to be married. He together with my other brothers send you their kind remembrance. Mrs. Rassam unites with me in much love to yourself and Mrs. Perkins, and your darling little Henry Martyn.

"Believe me, my dear sir, most sincerely yours,

"C. A. Rassam."

From Rev. Samuel A. Rhea, of Gawar, on his arrival at Oroomiah, in ill health.

"*Oroomiah, Sept. 25th*, 1852.

"My dear Brother and Sister, — I reached

here yesterday evening; and did I not feel weary and feeble, I would gladly ride up and spend an hour or two with you to-day.

"I would not, my beloved but deeply bereaved friends, even by allusion, rudely touch those tender chords, which I know still vibrate in the keenest anguish; but my attachment to dear departed Judith, the many pleasant hours spent with her, the no small share she added to my happiness in anticipated visits to Seir, and the sad and deeply grieved spirit with which I now visit it, give me the liberty to mention her name. My own feelings will find relief, though I have no hope that yours will. By this deeply and inexpressibly distressing event, with all its attending circumstances, I feel that God has placed you beyond the reach of our poor sympathies. Our hearts may bleed with yours, but we cannot heal the bleeding wounds. We can only sit in submissive silence, and feel, 'it is the Lord;' while we attempt, in our feeble but most heartfelt petitions, to beg for you the near presence of our tender, sympathizing Saviour. O I know you have already felt, and will continue to feel, under you, the arm of His love, sustaining you under a weight of sorrow that few are ever called to bear.

"My heart experienced a sudden transition from unspeakable grief to an overflowing joy, when I passed from the sad announcement of her death, to another line, which led me to believe, that your loved Judith is in heaven, a glorified spirit, resting sweetly on the bosom of her Saviour. Then I thought, 'Oh death, where is thy sting! Oh grave, where is thy victory!' How soon, if faithful, and we too shall be there; and His tender hand will wipe all tears from our eyes!

"I hope to see you soon, and till then, believe me to be your brother in Christ Jesus,

"S. A. Rhea."

The following note, from Deacon John Hormezd, the Nestorian pastor of Geog Tapa, who passed several years of his childhood in the family of Judith's parents, is inserted as a specimen of the kind sympathy, cherished and expressed by multitudes of their Nestorian friends. The note was written in Syriac, and is a literal translation, as will naturally be suggested by its style.

"To you, Mr. Perkins, my dear spiritual father, who brought me up with much care, in the hope of rearing in me a choice vine, by which sprouts and tendrils should be planted in desert places, that had no precious savor to sweeten their souls, which were seasoned with the evil customs and habits of their fathers, grown up, like themselves, without the instruction of blessed pious parents, and without the kind discipline of a disciple of Christ, our dear Saviour, who, in his tender love, made a scourge of small cords, with which he chastised those who were trading in the house of prayer:

"Be it known to you, that from the time of Judith's death, of whom I used to think as a beautiful scion and precious vine, my heart burns with sympathy for her dear parents — strangers in a strange land, who have left their dear native country, to gather the scattered ones of Zion in the region of Babylon.

"But it is delightful to me to think of *her* — to call her to remembrance, as a flower of April, that displays its beauty in its season, and as the rose of May, that gives forth its sweet odor during a pleasant month, and then its end comes, and it discontinues that sweet odor. Such was your dear daughter. Truly sweet was her voice, and pleasant her conversation, and gentle her life, and accomplished her character. Especially did I delight much to hear her play on the *seraphine*, which her hands plied as though she were a master, and had long practised. O how great was my pleasure, when I used to hear her playing, and listened to her sweet singing!

"I remember her well, when she was a little

child. She was very quiet, and smiling, and happy; not crying, and peevish, and wearisome to her parents and nurse.

"In the last years of her life, how humble and how peaceful was her walk! She always showed me great kindness, when I met her. *Malek Aga beg*, and many others, speak of her with much feeling — especially of her sweet music. We trust she is in heaven.

"Your sincere friend,

"JOHN."

Good priest Abraham, an early friend and missionary helper of Judith's parents, evinced his deep sympathy for them, and his heart-felt esteem for their loved daughter removed, some time after her death, by modestly and delicately intimating his desire, and that of his wife, to call their infant daughter by the cherished name of *Judith*; though that name was before unused among the Nestorians. They had selected two names, hitherto unused among their people, from which to choose, namely, *Judith*, and *Jane*, "the Young Cottager," the latter from the tract bearing that title, not long ago translated into the modern Syriac. Their choice strongly inclined to the former, in case the bereaved parents of Judith should have no objection to it; and all such apprehensions were of course soon removed, when those parents were apprized of their wishes on the subject.

A son of priest Abraham was with the afflicted family, on their sorrowful journey. He is a pious, interesting young man, seventeen years old, who started to accompany them to Erzroom, on his way to Malta, to become a member of the protestant college on that island. He, as well as the two Nestorian attendants on the road, was almost overcome by the affecting scenes which they witnessed; and so strong and mournful were the impressions which they made on his mind, and the minds of his parents, that they could never again bring their feelings to the trial of his going so far from home.

But very precious and blessed as well as melancholy, is the recollection of Judith's death, throughout the Nestorian community, as is indicated not only by their deep feelings of interest and sympathy expressed, but also by constantly occurring incidents. The children of a Nestorian Sabbath school, for instance, some time after that event, having repeated the hymn, commencing,

"How blest the righteous, when he dies," etc.,

were asked by their superintendent, whether they had ever known such a death; to which many little voices instantly responded, "Yes, *Judith's.*" The sweet savor of her precious memory will long exert a hallowed influence on multitudes of the Nestorians.

Another class in Persia — the Mohammedans — were not backward in the utterance of their tender sympathy for the stricken mourners. From no one did the parents of Judith receive a more hearty expression of condolence, than that addressed to them personally, by their long tried friend, Prince Malek Kâsem Meerza, one of the finest specimens of humanity in Persia, or any other land, who visited Oroomiah and Mount Seir, not long after their daughter's death. "You are fast growing old," said he to Judith's father, and feelingly added, "Rest assured that our grief has been inexpressible, since we heard of your affliction; but it is God's doing; His will must be done." Many others of that class have shown themselves equally anxious to comfort the sorrowing hearts and cheer the desolation of the bereaved ones. The Mohammedan acquaintances of the mission, the mass of whom are very friendly to them, must not be judged by the cruel inhospitality of the rude villagers of *Zorava*, to whom the missionaries were strangers. Happily human sympathy is not confined within the limits of Christianity, either real or nominal. "God hath made of one blood all nations of men, for to dwell on all the face of the earth;" and among the grateful proofs of the truth of this Scripture declaration, are remaining traces of a strong and genial common sympathy in them all, even among the most melancholy and deplorable ruins of the fall.

CHAPTER XIII.

NOTES OF CONDOLENCE CONTINUED.

(FROM MEMBERS OF OTHER MISSIONS.)

From Rev. J. Peabody, of Erzroom.

"*Erzroom*, *Sept.* 20*th*, 1852.

"MY DEAR BROTHER PERKINS, — We are greatly distressed for you, your dear wife, and surviving child. I do not know when we have been so much so. We do feel, that our Heavenly Father has laid his hand heavily upon you, and inflicted such a deep wound in your hearts, that it cannot soon be healed. We most sincerely sympathize with you, in the heavy stroke with which He has seen fit to visit you, in the removal of your dear only daughter, in circumstances so peculiarly trying. The Lord bind up your broken hearts, and heal your most painful wounds. To Him alone can we commend you, and this we try to do, every day. He alone can sustain and comfort you. This you well know; but, oh, how difficult to feel right, when overwhelmed with grief. Perhaps, in this very severe and mysterious bereavement, you can see nothing but clouds and darkness around the divine throne. But though you may walk in darkness now you shall soon see light. Truly, the features of God's providential dealings with you now are obscure and intricate; but what is now dark, shall soon be illumined; what is now intricate, shall soon be unravelled. It is true, that now Providence frowns upon you; but God, behind a frowning providence, hides a smiling face.

"That beloved daughter, we suppose, left her mountain home in perfect health. She doubtless anticipated a pleasant visit at Erzroom. We were delighted with the thought of a visit from you, with your family. O that the shafts of that destroying angel, that is making such havoc in Persia, might have been warded off from her! O that she might have been spared to you! We know that she was the light of your eyes and the joy of your hearts. But of this we may rest assured, that our Heavenly Father doeth all things well; that He does not willingly afflict the children of men; and that what we know not now, in regard to so trying an event, we shall know hereafter.

"In regard to the death of dear Judith, we have heard no particulars. Col. Williams wrote

Mr. Brant where it occurred, and the time her distressing sickness continued; nothing more. We feel a deep solicitude in regard to your health, and that of Mrs. Perkins and Henry. May the Lord preserve your lives, and the lives of all the families connected with you.

"The Cranes will remain here, till they receive word from Oroomiah.

"Please to present my kindest and most sympathizing regards to Mrs. Perkins and Henry.

"I remain with best wishes and prayers, your affectionate, sympathizing brother,

"J. PEABODY."

From Mrs. M. L. Peabody.

"*Erzroom, Sept. 20th*, 1852.

"MY DEAR BROTHER AND SISTER, — Need I assure you, that since we heard of your deep affliction, you have been in our thoughts day and night? Our tears have flowed with yours, and both at the family altar and in our private supplications, it has been our fervent prayer, that the balm of consolation may be poured into your wounded hearts. O my dear friends, in this, your sore trial, how poor would be all our attempts to comfort you! But you know there is One to whom you can go; He has wounded and he can heal.

"As yet we know scarcely any thing of that mournful event that snatched your darling Judith from your arms. All we have heard, is through a letter from Col. Williams to Mr. Brant. The tenderest sympathies of all seem strongly awakened for you, and to all of us it is a solemn admonition of Providence. O with how slight a tenure do we hold our dear children! How frail are our own lives! May this event lead us to think more of eternity and less of time!

"Our friends, Mr. and Mrs. Crane, and little Sarah Stoddard, are now with us. O how much pleasure were we promising ourselves in your society also, for a few weeks! A sadness is cast over all our little party.

"Do let me hear from you, my dear Mrs. Perkins, when you feel able to write. I am anxious to hear the particulars of that trying scene — the last words of your dear Judith. We trust her sweet spirit is now in heaven. Dear sister and brother, farewell. May the God of all consolation comfort you.

"Affectionately your sister,

"M. L. PEABODY."

The youthful reader may like to be told something respecting Erzroom, from which the foregoing letters were written. It is a large Turkish town, on a very elevated plain in Armenia, surrounded by lofty mountains. It is more than four hundred miles north-west from Oroomiah, and about two hundred miles due west from Mount Ararat. It is a very ancient town, near the head waters of the western branch of the river Euphrates, and was founded, as tradition says, by a grandson of Noah. It is the *Arz* or *Arze* of ancient times, and took the affix *room*, from its belonging, at one period, to the Greek empire of *Room*. It figures largely in Armenian history, and was for some time the capital of that ancient kingdom. The American Board of Missions commenced a station there for the Armenians in 1839. Mr. and Mrs. Peabody are, at the present time, the only missionaries at that station, where the good work is in cheering progress.

From Rev. P. O. Powers, of Trebizond.

"*Trebizond, Sept.* 28*th*, 1852.

"To Mr. and Mrs. Perkins:

"My dear Brother and Sister, — I scarcely know whether I should intrude myself upon your sorrows, or like the friends of Job, sit in silence at a distance and weep. But I cannot forbear expressing to you how deeply we have been afflicted, by the mournful intelligence that you have been bereaved of a beloved, an only daughter, and that under very trying circumstances.

We sympathize with you most sincerely, in this afflictive dispensation of divine Providence, and the earnest prayer of our heart is, that He who has wounded may make whole; that as the sources of earthly enjoyment dry up, you may have freer access to the great fountain head of a purer, richer, sweeter, more abiding and heavenly bliss. You are not strangers to affliction. Many times has our mother earth opened to swallow up your beloved offspring. I trust also that you are not strangers to the divine consolations of the gospel. Where shall any and all of us find relief, under the many and painful trials of this life, but in sweet submission to the hand that smites us! That same hand carries a healing virtue along with it. In vain do we look elsewhere for consolation.

"But you weep. So Jesus wept. He lets us also weep. It often relieves the throbbing heart. But it must be with such a quiet spirit of resignation as the Saviour felt. With what heavenly accents did he pronounce those blessed words, 'O my father, ... thy will be done.' These words he has put into our mouth. They become us, as well as the bleeding Saviour.

"I long to hear from your own pen how the Lord is dealing with you, and supporting you under your sorrows. I long also to know something of the particulars of dear Judith's death. Do gratify us, dear brother, so far as your feelings may allow you. Mrs. Powers desires to unite with me in every sentiment of grief and sympathy, and also in prayers to the Father of all our mercies in your behalf.

"With a kiss from each of us for your surviving Henry Martyn, and a renewed assurance of love and sympathy and a remembrance at the throne of grace, I am, dear brother and sister,

"Yours very truly and affectionately,

"P. O. Powers."

Trebizond, the place from which the preceding letter was written, is on the south-eastern shore of the Black Sea, about one hundred and fifty miles north-west of Erzroom, and six hundred miles east of Constantinople. It is the *Trapezus* of ancient times, in the province of ancient Pontus; where the Greek general and historian Xenophon, and his illustrious "*ten thousand*," reached the sea, and were welcomed by their countrymen, a Greek colony, on their renowned retreat from Babylon, after the defeat of the younger Cyrus. The American Board of Missions commenced a station there for the Armenians, in 1834. Mr. and Mrs. Powers are now the only missionaries at that station, where they are graciously prospered in their missionary work.

From Rev. H. G. O. Dwight, D. D., of Constantinople.

" *Constantinople*, (*Orta Keuy*,) *Oct.* 5*th*, 1852.

"My dear afflicted Brother and Sister,—I think it was nearly twelve years ago, that two little girls sat at our table, who were nearly of the same age, and both of whom were considered by their parents, and might have been considered by others, as uncommonly lovely and interesting. More than five years since, one of these, little Mary, was suddenly snatched away from her parents, and removed to a better world, as we have ever fondly hoped. The pang of sorrow, occasioned by this sudden and unexpected separation, is, to this day, remembered, and I may say, freshly felt, whenever the name of that loved one is mentioned, or her form appears before our mental vision.

"The other dear one, your own *dear Judith*, we have heard within the past week, has been taken from you, under circumstances of uncommon aggravation. It is one of those cases, in which, at first sight, it seems as though death, like a blood-thirsty tyrant, took pleasure not only in choosing a *shining mark*, but just such circumstances as would in the highest degree harrow up the feelings of surviving friends.

"The eye of Christian faith, however, sees the thing far differently. The event itself, with all the attending circumstances, whatever may be their nature or aggravation, has happened under the perfect and entire control, and by the wise orderings, of our kind Heavenly Father—the very best friend we have in all the universe. Of course there is no mistake in the thing; and no cruelty and no caprice.

"O how happy must you be now, if you can say from the bottom of your hearts, 'My Heavenly Father, who loves me with an infinite love, has done all this, and done it with the distinct end in view of promoting *my highest good!*' A higher end He has in all His acts, namely, *his own glory;* and it would seem that in each case, He chooses for us and ours, that kind of death which will most glorify Him. John, 21: 19. Most blessed of all must you be, if you have attained, by God's spirit, to that high elevation of obedience and submission, which enables you now to rejoice, even in the *manner* of your loved one's death, *because by that God was more glorified than he would have been by any other.*

"I am well aware, that it is a most difficult thing to say any thing, in such circumstances, that really meets the case; and oftentimes, in such deep sorrows, every thing that is offered by way of consolation, comes so far short of meeting the spot where most the wound is felt, that it better never have been said. In your case, however, I know from my own experience that the mere expression of that sympathy, which all your missionary brethren and sisters feel, and deeply feel, for you, will operate as a soothing balm to your wounded spirits, however impossible it may be for them to enter into the depths of your sorrows.

"Yes, my dear brother and sister, be assured, we all feel that *your* affliction is *ours;* and O how gladly would we do something, if we could, to lighten the burden of your griefs. We can only commend you to God, as we have done again and again, with bursting hearts, and we pray that God Himself may fill, with his own glorious presence, that 'aching void' in your hearts, which has been caused by the sudden removal of your beloved daughter.

"What a dark world would this be, without the gospel of Christ! But O, how happy is our lot, that we can look forward to a world of perfect brightness, where all the severed members of Christ will be gathered into one, and there will be no more separations, and no more interruption to our joys, to all eternity! May we and all ours be prepared to live together in that blessed world!

"Begging a remembrance in your prayers, I remain, my dear brother and sister,

"Very sincerely yours,

"H. G. O. Dwight."

From Mrs. M. L. Dwight.

"*Constantinople, Oct. 5th,* 1852.

"My dear Mrs. Perkins, — We have heard, through Col. Williams, of the overwhelming affliction with which you have been visited, and I cannot refrain from expressing my deep sympathy in your sorrow. I do not expect to be able to comfort you, but I may tell you that I weep with you, and I know from experience, that this is soothing to the breaking heart. My heart is drawn out to all bereaved mothers, since I have tasted the same bitter cup, and I must sympathize with them. But the circumstances of your bereavement were so trying, that they must have given double poignancy to your grief, and I should expect to hear that you were overwhelmed by the terrible blow, did I not know that the blessed Saviour is always present with His followers, and that His grace is sufficient for all circumstances. To His loving kindness we continually commend you, and your dear husband; and I trust that you are able, even now, to sing of mercy. O this sympathizing, tender Saviour!

How could we go through the deep waters without Him? I can only hope and pray, that He will manifest the fulness of His love to you, and then you will rejoice, even in this bitter sorrow.

"You have before experienced repeated bereavements; but I think our love for our children grows with their growth; if it is so with you, you will feel that your former afflictions were light, when compared to this. But God has revealed himself as the God of all consolation; and there is no sorrow so great, that He cannot comfort. O may he comfort you!

"I have a vivid remembrance of your dear departed daughter, as she was at the time you were here; and though, of course, time had made a great change in her, I still think of her as one with whom I was acquainted. She was so near the age of our loved departed one, that she is in a measure associated with her in my memory.

"We all long to know more than we yet know, of the circumstances of your dear child's departure; we long to know more of her; and we long to know how you are supported, in this sore trial.

"Please present my kind regards to Mr. Perkins, and assure him of my deep sympathy.

"Believe me to be, most truly, your friend and sister,

"M. L. Dwight."

Judith was seven years old, when she heard of the death of little Mary Dwight, who is referred to in the foregoing letters. She retained a vivid remembrance of her acquaintance with that lovely little missionary playmate, for a few days, though she had not seen her since they were less than three years old. The tidings of Mary's death deeply affected her. At the time, she fervently prayed that the bereaved parents might be comforted; and the departed one's name was often afterward mentioned by her, with tender and affectionate solemnity. How blessed the greeting of their happy, glorified spirits, in heaven!

From Rev. William G. Schauffler.

"*Bebek, Constantinople, Nov. 3d*, 1852.

"Rev. J. Perkins, D. D.:

"Dear Brother, — We have heard of your affliction with deep sympathy. We remembered the child you had to give up, and endeavored to realize how every year of growth and development must have added to the value of her society, and endeared her to you both, as she was more and more becoming a companion to you, in your family, comforts and trials, and in your labors. But we are aware, that only actual experience, the real surrender of a child of that age, can make us feel all the bitterness of such a cup; embittered still more, by the suddenness of the event, and the desolation, as to efficient means, advice, and assistance, in her treatment and comfort for her last hours.

"And has this stroke come from our blessed Jesus? Has he had the decision and disposal of that case, and has he chosen, that it be just so? Certainly. And now, is this event a proof of His unkindness, or unmindfulness of the weal or wo of His children? Or, is His undoubted kindness a proof, that this was the very best that even *He* could have done, both for the parents and the child? Certainly, the latter; whatever *we* may think, or however *our* feelings may rise, or break down, or melt, in view of such an event.

"But you will see her again; and I trust there, where parting scenes and farewell tears are unknown. Thus did Lowth write upon the gravestone of his beloved eldest daughter, Maria, "At veniet felicius ævum, quum iterum tecum, sim modo dignus, ero,"* etc.; and it will not be long either. Our days have wings, and these wings grow longer and mightier every day; and soon they will bear us over into the world of spirits, a time without time. Then earthly trou-

* "But a happier age will come, when with you again, if only I am worthy, I shall be," etc.

bles will appear a short dream, and our pangs in separating, a short, but very valuable preparation, for a happy and eternal reunion with all the friends of our blessed Saviour; and there, I trust, all our children will be present; the children of a covenant of peace, which will stand, though mountains should be removed, and hills be carried into the midst of the sea.

"We shall be glad to hear, that dear Mrs. Perkins has been sustained and comforted. A *mother's heart* is the tenderest spot of *humanity*. But the consolations of the gospel, applied by the spirit of grace, are sufficient even for that sorest spot of our nature.

"May the Lord be with you, with the richest, sweetest comforts within the stores of his love. And may your spiritual children be born as the dew of the morning for multitude, while your dear departed child is awaiting you in glory, where you shall come, bringing in your sheaves with you.

"Yours most truly,
"W. G. SCHAUFFLER."

From Rev. Cyrus Hamlin.

"*Bebek, Oct. 23d*, 1852.

"MY DEAR BROTHER AND SISTER, — The intelligence of your affliction filled our hearts with amazement and grief. It seemed like something which *could not* be true, the circumstances so heart-rending, the bereavement so sudden — so unlooked for, cutting down a cherished lovely daughter, in the fresh bloom of her years. All hearts have been drawn toward you, with a common sympathy. All have felt like weeping with those that weep, and at the same time, have felt how vain is human sympathy.

"Anguish of spirit will long attend the recollection of those few hours of suffering. Still, we must stop and remember, that our Heavenly Father did it. It formed a part of his perfectly wise, glorious, merciful, and holy plan of governing this world, and bringing his people home to glory. It was determined by infinite wisdom, in all its circumstances, in every thing that was accessory and preparatory to it.

"I trust you can also feel that that short, rough journey of a few hours ended in eternal rest. If so, this is enough. Any thing that ends in heaven, we will not repine. The flesh shrinks back, and we beseech our Father to let this cup pass from us; but He says, 'no; take it from my hand and drink it.' My sweet, precious little Mary gave me such a lesson, in her last sickness, as will always remain in my heart, through the changes of this dying world. I offered her a nauseous medicine; and having first tasted it myself, I said, 'Now I shall have to give this by force, every time it is administered.' She rejected it with pain and disgust, as I anticipated. I looked sternly at her, and said firmly, 'My little daughter *must take it.*' She gave me a look of momentary surprise, and then swallowed it down, and never afterward, (although she had to take it frequently for four days,) did she once refuse. It almost broke my heart. She was surrounded, two or three weeks, by prayer, and tenderness, and medical skill, day and night; and yet, she had as many hours of *dreadful suffering*, probably, as Judith did. Oh! there is a heaven for those we love. This thought was my stay, when giving up the sweet child. I doubt not it was yours. Is it not sufficient to make us silent, submissive, joyful, and happy, under the chastisements of our Heavenly Father!

"Henrietta has always remembered Judith with peculiar interest, and has felt her death deeply. I trust she also is a child of God, and if she should be taken from me, I should sorrow not as those without hope. She is the image of her sainted mother, has the same refinement and bashfulness of character. My four daughters are cherished treasures, but they are very insecure.

"Death has been very busy, of late, in the missionary ranks; Miss Whittlesey, Mrs. Morgan, Mr. Sutphen, Mary, Judith, — all within a short time have been taken from us. *Our* work is drawing toward its close, and how should we be straightened, until it is finished!

"Give much love to Mr. and Mrs. Stoddard, and to all your circle. Be assured, dear brother and sister, you are constantly remembered in our prayers, and have our deepest sympathies. The Lord strengthen you to glorify Him in this bereavement.

"Your affectionate brother,

"C. HAMLIN."

Not a few of the readers of this memoir will doubtless recognize, in the "sainted mother," referred to in the preceding letter, the female missionary, who died so peacefully and triumphantly, in her solitary situation, surrounded only by her stricken husband and five little daughters, (we mean, of *earthly friends*, for Jesus and the angels were there,) on the island of Rhodes, in November, 1851. They will also have in mind the baptism of the "little Mary," whose death is mentioned in this letter, in circumstances most tender and affecting, just before that mother's departure. "Henrietta," the eldest of the "four daughters," still remaining, was just about Judith's age, and was one of her loved playmates, during her short visit at Constantinople, on her return from America to Persia, whom she ever afterward remembered, with affectionate interest.

From Rev. N. Benjamin.

"*Constantinople, Nov. 23d*, 1852.

"Rev. J. Perkins, D. D.:

"My dear Brother, — No ordinary circumstances would have prevented my writing you, some weeks since, to assure you of our tenderest sympathy for yourself and dear Mrs. Perkins, in your late heavy trial. We received the first painful intelligence, when we were in the midst of our laborious preparations for removal to this city. After our arrival here, on the 22d ult., (not the most favorable season,) I was of course unceasingly occupied in searching for a house, and then in moving into it, when found. Meantime, I have been obliged to keep the printers supplied with copy, and look after the proofs, uninterruptedly.

"This delay in writing you, as I have had it in my heart to do, has permitted me first to see your account of the painful circumstances, in which you were called to part with the darling of your hearts, and of the blessed consolations with which the gracious Lord has supported you. It was indeed a heart-rending tale, and it broke up the fountain of our tears; but when I came to the close, every other feeling gave place to the feeling of thankfulness, for so sure a hope, that your beloved daughter has become a partaker of a blessed immortality. Yes, truly, our *every* affliction here is 'light,' when compared with *her* 'weight of glory,' which is already *exceeding*, and will be *eternal*. 'Thanks be unto God, for his unspeakable gift.'

"My dear brother, is it not a privilege to have children in heaven? I trust I have one there. He died an infant, but he is wiser than all philosophers and holier than all prophets and apostles ever were, in this world. May it be our happiness to join these dear ones, in the Lord's good time. Let us use all diligence *first to finish* our work.

"I feel nearer to you here than I did at Smyrna, and shall enjoy hearing from your mission more frequently and more particularly, than we have heretofore heard.

"The Lord has favored us much in our moving, the weather having been unusually fine, so that we still dispense with fires. I still carry on some printing at Smyrna, and hope soon to begin here.

"Mrs. B. desires with me much love to Mrs. Perkins, and to your little boy, as well as to yourself, and in the assurance of her tenderest sympathy. Please remember us kindly to all the friends at your station.

"Most truly yours,

"N. Benjamin."

Constantinople and its vicinity, from which several of the preceding notes were written, are doubtless well known, even to the youthful reader, especially to those familiar with the history of the glorious reformation in progress among the Armenians of Turkey. It was at the capital, that that reformation commenced, about twenty years ago, under the divine blessing on the labors of Messrs. Goodell, Dwight, and Schauffler, and it has rapidly radiated thence, in every direction, till its light has reached and blessed here and there a spot, not few, nor far between, to the remotest bounds of that great empire.

From Rev. S. H. Calhoun, of the Syrian mission, who was at Smyrna when he wrote.

"*Smyrna, Oct.* 16*th*, 1852.

"My dear Brother, — I have heard of your affliction, and cannot refrain from sending you and sister P. a word of sympathy. The event has saddened every heart among us. The circumstances of the death of your dear child were in the last degree distressing, so far away from home, and medical skill, and the presence of kindred spirits. But One was near, whose heart is love, and whose arm is power. In that solitary place, *He* was bending over you, and dealing with you, not as aliens, but as children; chastening, yet as a parent chasteneth his own son in whom he delighteth; wounding, yet only to bind up with his own band of tenderness.

" May you, my dear brother and sister, be supported in this hour of grief. May you find the promises sweet, and be enabled to repose on them. May you have such manifestations of our gracious Lord, that your hearts shall rejoice. I know that human words, at such times, are powerless; and yet I thought it might comfort you to know, that your brethren in the flesh are not unmindful of your sorrows, and bear you on their hearts to the throne of grace.

" I am here on my way to Syria, from Constantinople, where I have been spending a few weeks, in hope of recruiting my health, which has been considerably impaired during the past summer. Mrs. Calhoun would unite with me, (were she here,) in affectionate regards to Mrs. P. and yourself.

" Will you remember me fraternally to all your associates.

" Your ever affectionate brother in the Lord,

" S. H. CALHOUN."

The writer of the foregoing note, as is probably known to the reader, is stationed at Abieh, on Mount Lebanon — that "goodly mountain" of cedars, so often mentioned in the Psalms and other parts of the Bible. There he has a seminary, to train up Syrian youth, to become preachers of salvation, in the land where the Saviour labored, suffered, and died.

From Rev. Benjamin Schneider, of Aintab.

"*Aintab, Oct. 26th*, 1852.

"MY DEAR BROTHER AND SISTER PERKINS, — I snatch a few moments to send you a few expressions of condolence, in your recent sore bereavement. I have not seen Mr. Perkins's letter, or circular, containing the particulars; yet the bare fact of the sudden stroke, while travelling in these rude lands, far from the comforts and conveniences of home, must indeed be a trial. I sympathize with you, dear brother and sister. Though never called to drink so bitter a cup, I am a parent, and know well how keenly you must feel the stroke. But He who has wounded can also heal. As you are not mourners without hope, there is certainly great solace in the affliction. When I hear of the death of a child, my first query is, 'Was it probably a moral agent?' or, 'Did it give evidence of piety?' If these inquiries can be answered favorably, then I always feel like speaking words of consolation to the weeping mourners. And as you have such a hope, I understand, respecting your dear departed one, I would remind you of the *gain she* has found, in your *loss.* She is but gone before you, and you may expect soon to rejoin her. O if our children are but safe, through grace, safe while living, and saved when dying, I feel that it is comparatively of little moment, whether they are with us a longer or shorter time. If they and we are but gathered at last, into the great family above, what matters it which go first? How soon we shall all follow those who have preceded us! They are going one after another, and some of those we love must go before us.

"I know your hearts will bleed; for it is not the first bereavement. But, dear brother and sister, remember that it is the hand of *love* that has smitten; and you will one day see, how an event, so trying in its nature, could have been all in mercy. The Lord be your consolation and comfort.

"You have doubtless heard, that Mrs. Schneider, and our two daughters, and two of our sons, have gone to America, the youngest remaining with me. They have arrived safely, and had a blessing on the voyage. Mrs. S. found her aged parents still living, and overjoyed to see her and her children.

"Much love to all your missionary circle.

"Yours most truly,

"B. SCHNEIDER."

Aintab, the Turkish town from which this note was written, is in the south-eastern part of Asia Minor, some forty or fifty miles north of Aleppo, in Syria. Its name, in Arabic, signifies "good spring," and is applied to the place, on account of the many fine springs of water in the vicinity of the town. It is at present the scene of a reformation, among the Armenian inhabitants, more rapid in its progress and interesting in its character, than in any other part of the Armenian field.

From Rev. W. F. Williams, of Mosul.

"*Mosul, Oct. 2d*, 1852.

"MY DEAR AFFLICTED BROTHER, — How sad a budget came to our hands, by the messenger this time! How deeply I sympathize with you, in this your desolating bereavement, you yourself already know; for you too acknowledge the same injunction, to 'weep with those that weep, and rejoice with those who rejoice.'

"Of the loved one departed, I know only the name and the narrative of your 'memorandum;' but it does not need a personal acquaintance in order to stir up the deep fountains of sympathy. Though in the flesh a stranger to you all, with no idea of form or feature, figure or face, yet to the mind's eye, you each and all are individualities, personalities, not simply fragments of aggregate humanity; and in my heart's warmth, you each have a place. And though the shape of room, the contour of externalities, lie indistinct and undefined, there yet is before me a vivid picture of *a family desolate,* (oh what meaning that one word carries, *desolate,*) a place vacant; hearts yearning after that they no more reach; anguish welling up and overflowing at sight of some remembrance — some object, so linked with the absent one as to be forever and indelibly associated.

"I see a landscape lying just before you in the future, all sunshine and joy; hill and dell, with flowing glen, around which cluster all pleasant hopes and fond anticipations; amid which shall gently pass life's closing labors and ending scenes; and lo! at its very entrance, it is overcast with portentous clouds, and in an instant, there remains only *desolation.* That pleasant prospect, opening into the future, is annihilated. And yet I hear from the lowest depths of your stricken soul, 'It is well;' for He hath done it who 'doeth all things well.' This is the Christian's confidence in his God, his Father; 'Though He slay me, yet will I trust in Him.' The earthly paradise is exchanged for a heavenly. That which was so sweet to hope in the future — the decline of life — is cheerfully resigned, the soul borne up, sustained, nay more, is triumphant, in the certain assurance, that it is but for a time the vision fades, that it may reappear, purer, brighter, *eternal.*

"We *know* in whom we have believed; and that He is able to keep that which we have committed unto Him, against 'the judgment of the great day;' and so your loss becomes not only *her*, but *your* gain, because 'it worketh for you the peaceable fruits of righteousness;' since 'all things work together for good to them who love God;' and most of all, 'these light afflictions which endure but for a moment,' in comparison with 'the far more exceeding and eternal weight of glory,' to which they point our eyes.

"Thus are all things true blessings to the Christian; and here only is the value of human sympathy in bereavement, in that with us it lifts the tearful eye to the cross of Christ; and doing this, how precious is its kindness, how tender and soothing its power! May He, who has given you this effective proof of sonship, in that He has taken from you your idol, your beloved, in that He has counted you worthy of chastisement, in the same love spare to you your remaining child, and gladden your hearts by permitting you to see him eminently useful in the Master's vineyard, and at length gather you all—'a whole family in heaven.'

"With hearty sympathy and good wishes I must close.

"Yours,

"W. F. WILLIAMS."

Mosul, from which the preceding letter was written, is situated on the western bank of the river Tigris, just opposite the ruins of ancient Nineveh, whose marble palaces are now in process of excavation under the direction of Col. Rawlinson, and whose records, inscribed on the vast marble tablets that line the halls of those palaces, afford astonishly interesting confirmation of the Holy Scriptures; for instance, records of the impious Sennacherib's attempted invasion of Jerusalem, in the days of king Hezekiah. This ancient capital of the "Assyrian empire," is now the seat of "the Assyrian mission" of the American Board, to the Jacobites, and the "Chaldeans," i. e. the Papal Nestorians.

In this chapter, we have thus accidentally performed a hasty circuit, starting from Oroomiah and proceeding north-west to the Black Sea, westward to Constantinople, thence southward to Syria, and thence back eastward to the Tigris, to the station nearest to the Nestorian mission, about three hundred miles distant from Judith's home. We have introduced the notes of condolence, from deeply sympathizing missionary fellow-laborers, on this long circuit of thousands of miles, that were written within a few weeks, and happened to reach her stricken parents within three months after her death, in a country where there is neither electro-magnetic telegraph, nor steam, and only a monthly English mail, carried by a horseman, to enable them to communicate with those distant stations and with the civilized world. Another three months would doubtless add many to the list of these affectingly interesting epistles, from brethren and sisters at the same or still other stations. Enough, however, have been introduced, to impress the reader with the truth, that there is a blessed reality in "the communion of saints," far enough from the pale of Roman Catholic exclusion, or Puseyite assumption, — that there is a cord of sympathy and love, that binds together the hearts of believers, and especially of missionaries, whether known or unknown personally to each other, as sensitive as the electric wire, and infinitely more stable, enduring, and sure; and a cord, so far from being limited to any single circuit like the one here embraced, which extends to earth's extremest bounds, wherever a child of God is found, and upward to the heart of Christ, its centre and its source.

Such was the cord of sympathy and interest, by which Judith was encircled while she lived, and such is the cord which so tenderly vibrates for the bleeding hearts of her parents, when touched by the tidings of her death. How strikingly and how beautifully is the apostolic declaration here illustrated, that if "one member" of the Saviour's body "suffer, all the members suffer with it."

CHAPTER XIV.

CONCLUSION.

WE have mentioned the estimation in which Judith was held by the Nestorians, and have alluded particularly to her interest in the Female Seminary, and the place she occupied in the hearts of its pupils. And it is perhaps appropriate, that one at least of the *females* of the people among whom she was born and dwelt, for whose salvation she longed and prayed, and, so far as a child could do it, labored, and by whom she was so tenderly beloved, should be allowed, in her own way, to testify her regard for Judith, in this memoir. The following is a letter of condolence from one of the pupils of the Nestorian Female Seminary, to the bereaved parents. The writer is *Nargis*, whose name, in the languages of Persia, is the name of a favorite garden flower, and in this instance, very aptly characterizes the lovely, refined young lady who bears it. Having heard of Henry's using the expression in regard to his departed sister, "*she will rise again,*" Nargis worked that expression neatly on a book-mark for his Bible, and sent it to him with her letter to his parents. The letter, though long, is of too touching interest to weary the reader. It was written in Syriac, and is translated as literally as a readable translation would bear. The writer is a member of the senior class in the seminary, who spent the last summer of Judith's life in Gavalan, and was there, when her lifeless remains passed that village on the way to their last resting-place.

From Nargis.

"DEAR MR. AND MRS. PERKINS,—For a long time I have had it in my heart, with melancholy thoughts and mournful pen, and paper laden with sadness, to make known to you, how much I have shared with you in your bitter grief and painful sorrows; for whom? oh, how can I mention her name! for your daughter, snatched so suddenly from your midst! But I have not ventured to do it, and thus it has remained until Miss Fisk encouraged me to write you.

"Although it is very painful to call to remembrance the lamented death of that dear friend, who has gone to return not again,—who has been taken from the midst of us and will appear here no more, I still desire to write you respecting her, especially, when I remember how she used to speak of her love for her parents, and know, that if it be that she is looking down from heaven, she would greatly rejoice, should I write something that would contribute, even a little, to comfort the broken hearts of her parents whom she so much loved.

"My beloved friends, Mr. and Mrs. Perkins, perhaps you are not aware, that for the last four years, and more, I have cherished a peculiar love and friendship for Judith, and she for me; and though several months have passed since she died, it still seems to me as though it were this very minute. O that you knew how deep is my grief for her, my sorrow and my sadness! When I look on her notes which are with me, I cannot restrain my tears; and when I call her to remembrance, I cannot keep my mind from thinking of her. Very often, she is, as it were, before my eyes, entering the girls' seminary, with the deportment of a grown up lady. I remember with what light footsteps she would go to her place; and I call to mind how, on the wings of application, she would go forward with her lessons; and I forget not her reading in the first class — how we were astonished at her learning the Syriac language.

"Truly hard and bitter is it for me, to call to remembrance the removal of a friend so beloved. Yes, and it wounds my heart when I look upon you, her parents, when you come to the city, but *Judith* not with you; and when I behold her brother, and *no sister* with him; and when I see the children of the missionaries going to school, but *Judith* cometh not; for she has finished her studies forever. The Lord comfort your hearts, ye afflicted parents.

"Dear missionaries from America, I have thought, that perhaps you would like to have me tell you some things which I have observed in Judith. During the last year, I have not seen her much, except occasionally; but one thing which I have seen in her is this; in other years, although Judith was very exemplary, and had learned good habits, yet she seemed to have only the form of Christianity; but the past year, she has appeared as though pictured before the eyes of all the girls of the seminary, and a perfect model of a Christian has been seen in her. This was evident to us from her walk and conversation, and from her love to others, and her consistent character. Blessed are the parents who have such a daughter as she, prepared to dwell in heaven, with the Father and the Son!

"O ye stricken parents, your sweet daughter is before my eyes, when she came to Gavalan to meet Miss Harris. Alas, she knew not how soon she would sadden her! And before my vision is that delicate form, when she went out to walk with the girls on the hills of Gavalan. And when we tried to see who would first reach the tops of those hills, that little girl, in her nimble activity, was up as soon as the Nestorian girls. Oh, I remember the time, when she came to go on that journey which was so deeply to distress her parents. I remember how rejoiced I was, when I heard that *Judith* had come. After a little time, I entered the room and saw Judith there, and we kissed each other. We thought not that it was our *last* kiss.

" The last morning, when you were to depart, Judith rose earlier than the Nestorian girls, and came upon the terrace just as I was getting up. She waked the girls, saying that Miss Fisk desired them to rise. I said, 'Judith, why have you risen so early?' She joyously answered, 'that I may be ready to go.' I remember, when I said to her, 'Will you call and see us again?' so wakeful was her conscience, that she recollected her father's word and said, 'No, my papa gave me permission to go *now* wherever I wish; so I have come to see you now.' We conversed a little while about her going to America after some years, and she said, 'If it may be that I come here again, I will labor for the Nestorians, *where there are no laborers*." Oh, that was our *last* conversation until death!

"Dear friends, that Sabbath day, when the

letter was brought to Mr. Stocking, conveying the intelligence of her death, I little thought that she whom I so much loved would be separated from me all the days of my life. Oh, what anguish I felt on that day! With longing, I said to myself, 'would that I were even now with Judith!' The following night seemed very long to me; and when I rose on the morning of Monday, and it was said, 'they are coming,' in deep distress I stood, to see if indeed Judith had died that strange death. Suddenly, her parents entered, *without their daughter!* How bitter was that sight! And now came that delicate damsel, borne as the dead are borne, in company with the attendants. O beloved parents of Judith, if my failing pen should make the attempt, it could not express my anguish at that time! It was so hard for me to believe that she was really dead, that I requested Miss Fisk, that if it were possible, we might be permitted to see her. So we went to the tent of the dear dead one, which was pitched without, away from the friends, and I stood at her head and wept. It still seemed to me that that same rosy countenance was speaking to me; and with a heavy heart, I asked Miss Fisk, if we could not see her face. Gently replying, she said, 'That rosy face which you have seen, remains no longer.' Deep anguish seized me, and I went straight away, remembering the steps over which *Judith* had walked, and with difficulty could I again look in the direction where that tent was pitched.

"Beloved friends, hearing about the village near which you encamped, almost made me say, let the name of the place be blotted out, which had not in it *one merciful man*, in the time of a stranger's death.

"But how delightful is now the remembrance of the mountains of Ararat, when I recollect that *Judith* rejoiced over them. I implore the winds of the mountains of Ararat, to blow gently on the last foot-tracks of beloved Judith! And I entreat that morning star, on which *Judith* looked with such delight, that its sparkling rays may fall tenderly on her peaceful grave.

"Gone is the loved girl! Her life is now woven into the warp of eternity! Her face we shall see no more on earth!

"True it is, that deep is your grief. Your sorrow is like the sorrow of Jeremiah, and your endurance like the patience of Job. May Jehovah, who healed the sorrows of David, heal your sore wounds!

"Stricken parents, bereft of your daughter, submissive under the hand of Him for whose sake you have come from one end of the world to the other, I hope you will accept *this book-mark*, for your dear only son Henry, to place in his Bible. Please let him put it in the place where you read together, when you assemble around the family altar; when you are all seated, each in his chair, but *one seat is empty;* when you read, but *her sweet voice is not heard.* When you thus kneel down, and *she is not with you*, let this book-mark remind her little brother, that SHE WILL RISE AGAIN. Yes, that day for which he longed, he will behold, when the Saviour of the lost shall raise up again his sister, with eternal joy.

"Dear Mr. and Mrs. Perkins, sojourners in a stranger land, our hearts will still go out with yours, and our sorrow with your sorrow. Truly, dear friends, it causes our hearts to melt, when we think how great a distance, how many miles and leagues, intervene between you and your loved native country. We know that it would have been pleasant for you to have remained there, surrounded by loving friends. But 'I AM' will not forget your self-denials, and your love for the lost; and though your children, like faded flowers, lie scattered around you, the Lord Almighty will certainly gather them from every place where they are buried; and He will multiply to you children from among the Nestorians, and make them a company of the redeemed, prepared to dwell in heaven forever. And then you, with your assembled family, will commence singing the song of Moses, and the Lamb that was slain; and that day is near at hand.

"From your sorrowing friend,

"NARGIS."

In a note from Miss Fisk to Judith's father, which accompanied the foregoing letter, she says, "It has been a very great gratification to *Nargis* to be allowed to write you. Her love for our dear Judith was very strong, and she never speaks of her without tears. Her idea of Judith's Christian character is her own, and not in any way derived from us. Other girls feel just as she does, and it is pleasant to see them feel so. They do not make hers a death-bed repentance; and I feel that their testimony to her love of Christian conversation, is very delightful evidence that she carried a *Saviour* ever with her."

A few days after the return of the bereaved family, from the fatal journey, to their desolate home, Mr. Stoddard started for Erzroom, to meet Mr. and Mrs. Crane, and his little daughter. Near the place of Judith's death, he wrote the following note to her parents.

"*Near Zorava, Sept. 17th*, 1852.

"MY AFFLICTED BROTHER AND SISTER, — You have scarcely been out of my mind, all day long.

On leaving the caravanserai, this morning, to pursue my journey, my eyes immediately fell on the spring, where you, with Judith and Henry, sat down to eat your breakfast, just two weeks ago. As I wound my way up the mountain, I thought of Judith's impatience, as she went over the same road, to see the 'father of mountains.' And when I reached the top, and the fatal road lay mapped out at my feet, my heart was full, and I could only say over and over again, 'God comfort my dear brother and sister.'

"We descended the mountain, remembering with what elastic step Judith descended the same declivity. Both Hormezd and the muleteer pointed out the rock, near which you stopped, the last time, and took some refreshment. Afterwards, Hormezd spoke out suddenly, as I was riding in advance, and said, 'Here Judith first knew that she had the cholera.' From that place to *Zorava*, is a long and weary way, and I could imagine how anxiously your eyes traced out one turn after another, in hope that you would soon reach the village. I saw, as I passed, almost with shuddering, the fatal spot where you hung over the dying bed of Judith, and resigned her to Him who called her from your arms. I would have stopped at *Zorava* for the night, and meditated and prayed on that melancholy yet now hallowed spot; but I remembered the cruelty of the villagers to you, in your time of distress, and turned hastily away.

"Be assured, dear brother and sister, you have my constant sympathy and my earnest prayers. I cannot comfort you myself, but I can refer you to the true source of consolation. Go to the Saviour, and He will wipe away your tears, and fill you with sweet peace.

"Yours affectionately,

"D. T. Stoddard."

At Erzroom, Mr. Stoddard, in writing to Dr. Anderson, Secretary of the American Board of Commissioners for Foreign Missions, alludes thus to Judith's death. "The very affecting narrative which accompanies this, will inform you, far better than I can do, of the severe affliction of our dear brother and sister, Mr. and Mrs. Perkins. It can hardly be read without deep emotion.

"The loss of a child is always a heavy stroke; and no one can feel it more keenly than the missionary. Removed from father and mother, and the pleasant associations of home and country, he cherishes a very peculiar affection for his wife and children, which few in other circumstances can fully understand. Our brother and sister have five times before consigned children to the tomb. Their present affliction, however, comes in a new and very aggravated form. Their other children died in infancy; Judith, just as she was unfolding in beauty and maturity. The others died at their own home, where all was done for them which the physician's skill and parental love could suggest. The removal of Judith from them was very different. She was far from home, surrounded by unfeeling Mohammedans, attacked, and in a few hours borne down, by a fearful disease, with no physician to attend her, and only the shelter of a damp, cold tent, to shield her in her dying moments.

"Every thing in the external circumstances seemed to add intensity to the cup of affliction, to press these bereaved parents to the dust. And yet grace — that wonderful grace which God gives his children in time of need — has carried them with patience and resignation through this trial; and so far from murmuring, they bless God for his love to them, and to their beloved Judith, when the waves of sorrow were sweeping over them. Still, they cannot but feel deeply their loss. The light of their dwelling has been taken away; and in the twentieth year of their missionary life, they are left with only one survivor from their seven children. I need not say, that in these circumstances, they have our tenderest sympathy and most earnest prayers."

The following note was addressed to Judith's father, by Mr. Stevens, British consul at Tabreez, after reading a brief sketch giving account of her sickness and death.

"*Oroomiah, Oct. 29th*, 1852.

"Rev. Dr. Perkins:

"My dear Sir,—I return to you the memorandum you were so kind as to send me, which reached me after my arrival in Oroomiah. I have perused it with a mixture of regret and admiration—with regret for the sad loss—the irreparable loss—you have experienced; and with admiration of the truly Christian resignation, with which my dear departed friend submitted to the will of the Almighty.

"I fervently pray, that when it may please Him to call me away from this world, I may be prepared to obey the summons, with one tenth part of that quiet and religious submission, displayed by poor Judith, and which it was natural to expect, both from her own good qualities, and from the exemplary manner in which she had been reared by her now bereaved parents.

"I beg you will offer my respectful compliments to Mrs. Perkins, and that you will believe me, with my best wishes for you both,

"Yours very sincerely,

"R. W. Stevens."

From Mrs. A. E. Crane, written the day after her arrival at Oroomiah.

"*Oroomiah, Thursday morning, Oct. 21st*, 1852.

"My dear Mrs. Perkins, — After the first emotions of joy, on reaching our *long anticipated field and home*, our thoughts and sympathies turn to that dear brother and sister, who had so kindly purposed to come and accompany us hither from Erzroom. Instead of all the happiness we might have enjoyed, a bereavement so afflictive has fallen not only on you, but on *us all*, that we may well mourn together the loss of your beloved Judith. I would endeavor, my dear sister, to speak words of comfort and consolation, but cannot express my feelings; *words are too cold.* Only our Saviour, who wept with those that weep, can bind up your breaking hearts.

"We have had our feelings very tenderly called out, within the last few days, in passing places associated with the last hours of your sainted daughter. O that the same grace, that brightened and sustained her last hours, may illumine those benighted villages! If her death may be the means of quickening those of us who remain, in efforts for the *good of souls*, will it not be sanctified? May it not be to the greater glory of God our Father? Yes; while we mourn, it is 'not as those who have no hope.'

'It is the Lord. Let him do what seemeth him good.' May the presence of the Comforter be constantly with you, my dear sister. I hope to see you soon. With kindest regards to Mr. Perkins, and love to little Henry, in which Mr. Crane unites,

"In haste, but very affectionately yours,

"A. E. Crane."

From Mrs. S. A. Breath, accompanied by the beautiful stanzas which follow the note.

"*Oroomiah, Oct. 15th,* 1852.

"Mr. and Mrs. Perkins:

"Dear Brother and Sister, — I need not say, that I deeply sympathize with you; hard were the heart that did not feel. But sorrow such as yours is a sacred thing, and an awe is on my spirit. I have felt that any attempt to express sympathy, could but call forth the touching plaint, 'Is there any sorrow like unto my sorrow?' He who kills and makes alive, alone can heal such wounds as yours.

"The accompanying lines are intended only for your own perusal. You will, I know, overlook their faults, and accept them as an expression of sympathy,

"From your sister in Christ,

"S. A. Breath."

"TO MR. AND MRS. PERKINS.

"As one by one your little band
Have hastened to the spirit land,
How oft have you been called to shed
A parent's tears o'er the early dead;
To see the babe its eyelids close,
And fold its arms for a long repose;
But never have you felt a blow,
Like that which laid your JUDITH low.

"Parental joy your hearts would warm,
To note the unfolding mind and form;
To see a daughter's loving care,
Seeking a mother's toils to share;
Watching, when ill, beside her bed, —
A star's mild light on her pathway shed, —
Your toils and pains forgot the while,
Blest with the sunlight of her smile.

"How sweet in song her voice would rove;
How soft the strains her touch would move;
Our little circle gathered round,
Dwelt with delight upon the sound,
And caught the soul-inspiring lay,
Which bears the thoughts from earth away;
Now the soft notes a Saviour's love repeat —
And now, triumphant strains His coming greet.

"When at the placid hour of even,
Your cares are left, to think on heaven,
Do not your spirits catch the strains
Which float along celestial plains?
Does there not bend a listening ear,
Your absent loved one's voice to hear?
Her touch an angel's harp can make
With melodies of heaven awake.

"Dark is your path; yet one bright ray,
Remains to cheer you on your way;
Torn are your hearts; yet one fond hope
Is left to bear your spirits up.
Each day, each moment, brings more near,
The time when you with joy shall hear,
Their welcome who have gone before;
How blest to meet, and part no more."

Second note from Mrs. Breath, to Judith's mother, and lines which accompanied the note.

"DEAR SISTER,—I am alone with my little ones. You too are probably alone, but uncheered by the smiles of infancy. I have been thinking of you the more, to-day, from having read in the Journal of Missions the account of the sickness and death of dear Judith, with its attendant circumstances. As my mind rested on the melancholy theme, fancying myself in your place, my thoughts took the turn which I have expressed in a few lines. However poor the sympathy friends may offer, I know that you will not undervalue it. You are willing they should tell you they think of you and feel for you.

"Yours,

"S. A. BREATH."

"TO MRS. PERKINS.

"I will not weep, — though one by one
My treasures from my side have gone,
E'er she who was my hope, my aid,
Beside my youngest babe was laid.
I shall rejoin them in the sky;
Then why should tear-drops fill my eye?

"I will not weep — though o'er her head
The sun its noon-tide ray may shed,
And winter's fiercest tempests rave
About my darling's lonely grave.
'Twill not disturb her sweet repose;
And yet the tear unbidden flows.

"I will not weep — my bleeding heart,
Thy throbbing cease! 'Twas pain to part;
But, oh! 'tis bliss untold to know,
That far beyond this world of woe,
I yet shall meet my *Judith* dear,
Where sorrow never prompts a tear.

"I will not weep — no tears shall dim
My upward gaze. My hope in Him,
Who triumphed o'er the last dread foe,
Through His free grace, no doubts shall know.
In sorrow's night, I'll wait the day,
And wipe the flowing tears away."

Our melancholy but still grateful task, we now bring to a close. Our humble aim, which was but honestly and briefly to portray the lovely "Persian Flower," that has faded, — nay, rather that has been transplanted to the garden of God, with such incidental references as grow out of the subject and illustrate it, is fulfilled,—imperfectly indeed, yet, we trust, in a manner, that may contribute to comfort the stricken mourner, (as the task itself of preparing this brief record has done,) and interest, and, with the Divine blessing, benefit the general reader.

Would we look for human loveliness and promise? We have here presented one of the brightest and fairest samples. Would we contemplate mortal frailty? We have here a most impressive demonstration, that "the flower fadeth," and that most suddenly and unexpectedly. Would we look away from earth to heaven, from the present scene of change, disappointment, and sorrow, to those everlasting mansions of unalloyed joy and bliss, in reserve for all who love God? How affectingly beautiful and instructive, though so deeply afflictive to bereaved friends, was the calm and happy passage of young Judith to that world of glory, rapid as was that passage, and under the sudden summons of one of the most fearful of mortal maladies! Her remark to her little brother, uttered less than one week before her death, proved prophetic: "Perhaps I shall die on this journey; and how delightful it will be to go up to that heaven, and see God who never dies!"

May the reader, like her, seek and obtain a

place in that "house not made with hands, eternal in the heavens;" where "there shall be no more death; neither sorrow; neither crying; neither shall there be any more pain."

Just as we were penning the above last lines, a package of seven volumes of the published works of Dr. Geo. W. Bethune reached Judith's father, sent to him as a token of fraternal remembrance from that kind friend. In turning over the volume of his sweet "Lays of Love and Faith," the charming piece, "Early lost, Early saved," was one of the first to which we opened; and it struck us as so descriptive of the life and character of Judith, that we could not forbear to introduce it, as a most appropriate close of her memoir.

EARLY LOST, EARLY SAVED.

By Dr. Geo. W. Bethune.

Within her downy cradle, there lay a little child,
And a group of hovering angels unseen upon her smiled;
When a strife rose among them, a loving, holy strife,
Which should shed the richest blessing over the new-born life.

One breathed upon her features, and the babe in beauty grew,
With a cheek like morning's blushes, and an eye of azure hue;
Till every one who saw her, were thankful for the sight
Of a face so sweet and radiant, with ever fresh delight.

Another gave her accents, and a voice as musical
As a spring-bird's joyous carol, or a rippling streamet's fall;

Till all who heard her laughing, or her words of childish grace,
Loved as much to listen to her, as to look upon her face.

Another brought from heaven a clear and gentle mind,
And within the lovely casket the precious gem enshrined;
Till all who knew her, wondered, that God should be so good,
As to bless, with such a spirit, a world so cold and rude.

Thus did she grow in beauty, in melody, and truth,
The budding of her childhood just opening into youth;
And to our hearts yet dearer, every moment than before,
She became, though we thought fondly, heart could not love
her more.

Then spake out another angel, nobler, brighter than the rest,
As with strong arm, but tender, he caught her to his breast:
"Ye have made her all too lovely for a child of mortal race,
But no shade of human sorrow shall darken o'er her face;

"Ye have tuned to gladness only the accents of her tongue,
And no wail of human anguish shall from her lips be wrung;
Nor shall the soul that shineth so purely from within
Her form of earth-born frailty, ever know a sense of sin.

"Lulled in my faithful bosom, I will bear her far away,
Where there is no sin, nor anguish, nor sorrow, nor decay;
And mine a boon more glorious than all your gifts shall be —
Lo! I crown her happy spirit with immortality!"

Then on his heart our darling yielded up her gentle breath,
For the stronger, brighter angel, who loved her best, was
DEATH.

www.ingramcontent.com/pod-product-compliance
Lightning Source LLC
LaVergne TN
LVHW012328100826
845148LV00017B/396

* 9 7 8 1 4 2 5 5 2 1 3 7 0 *